Mothers & Daughters

Mothers & Daughters Anthology II

Text Copyright © 2023 by Annette Beggarly, Kim Clarkson-Elliott
Carolyn Lumpkin, Shandrika Milligan, Sabrina R. Owens

All rights reserved. No part of this book may be reproduced, scanned, or distributed in any printed or electronic form or by any means without prior written consent of the publisher, except for brief quotes used in reviews.

Please do not participate in or encourage piracy of copyrighted materials in violation of the author's rights. Purchase only authorized editions.

ISBN: 9798392555161

Printed in the United States

Fearless

Joan Oby Dawson

Copyright © 2024

All Rights Reserved

ISBN:

'Joan Oby Dawson' is to be identified as the author of this work.

No part of this publication may be reproduced or transmitted in any form or by any means, electronic or mechanical, including photocopy, recording, or any information storage and retrieval system, without permission in writing from the author.

Dedication

First and foremost, I thank my Lord and Savior, Jesus Christ, for allowing me to use the gifts He has given me to create. I pray that the words and stories in this short book are a blessing.

To my children, grandchild, and great-grandchild who continue to encourage me, Tandra, Paul, Nikki, Taymar, Horace, Tish, Lisa, and Tiffany, and the rest of the members of my extremely large family, you have always been supportive even as I grow older and more determined to "do it my way." You continue to love me and just be there when I need you. You embrace my choices of fashion, jewelry, lifestyle, and my determination to chart my own course. You, my family, are still there, smiling and listening to my long stories of life and steadfast faith.

Paul, our conversations when you visit are so important to me. Just your presence and encouraging words provide strength and peace. Michael, your editing helped tremendously. Thank you, Jacqui, for your thoughts and suggestions. Thank you, Cynthia, for being a constant companion and help. Your strong presence in my life keeps me young and vibrant.

To Dr. Kayode Williams of Johns Hopkins Hospital, my excellent pain doctor who made me promise to write

after I questioned him about his treatment and his explanation of "arthritis." I am a bit beyond the schedule you gave me; however, it is better late than never. Thank you.

Finally, Tandra, thank you for your invaluable input to help me make sense of my thoughts and ideas in shaping this writing. Your contribution is invaluable. I love you. You, too, are a beautiful, brilliant young woman. In fact, all of my children, my one grandchild, and my great-grandchild are brilliant, blessed, and beautiful. Y'all got it goin' on!!

Table of Contents

Dedication iii
About the Author vi
Chapter I Brand New 1
Chapter II Time 6
Chapter III Love 12
Chapter IV Heritage 19
Chapter V Dirt 28
Chapter VI Qualified 32
Chapter VII Influence 39
Chapter VIII Innocence 41
Chapter IX Chances 45
Chapter X Changes 53
Chapter XI Family 58
Chapter XII Courage 63
Chapter XIII Purpose 72
Chapter XIV Friendship 83
Chapter XV Boldness 92
Chapter XVI Light and Easy 100
Chapter XVII Giving 114
Chapter XVIII Understanding 122
Chapter XIX Life 133

About the Author

Dr. Joan Oby Dawson has a Ph.D. in Educational Administration from New York University, concentrating o*n Public School Administration and Supervision. She has National Certification with the American Speech-Language-Hearing Association a Master's* degree *in Speech Pathology and Audiology, specializing in Speech Pathology. She has over 50 years of experience in these areas.*

She *is also the author of* Look Up, an inspirational book on life and Multicultural Education: A History of Policy Development for the New York City Public Schools, from *1985 to 1995* (d*octoral study).*

Dr. Dawson has served on several Boards throughout the City of New York, including:

- Roosevelt Island Operating Board.
- Manhattan Community Board
- Mount Morris Community Association
- Community Pride, Harlem Children's Zone, Harlem Commonwealth Council
- National Board of The Transition Network, an organization that addresses issues of women over age 50.

- Founding Chapter of the New York Coalition of One Hundred Black Women.
- Chairperson of the Board of Harlem Commonwealth Council
- Chairperson of the Board of Harlem Congregations for Community Improvement.

Her accomplishments include:

- Recipient – AASA S.D. Shanklin Scholarship Award
- Recipient – Manhattan Community Board 10 Distinguished Service Award
- U.S. Department of Education Certificate of Appreciation for Improving America's Schools Regional Planning Committee, 1997, 1998, 1999, 2000, 2001
- Certificate for NCLB Implementation and Technical Assistance for Parents in Harlem Community
- Certificate of Appreciation, New York City Department of Education, Local Education Opportunity Coordinator Training Sessions, 2001
- Recipient – Governor's African American Community Service Award, February 2003
- Recipient – Judge's Award for Women in Black mentoring program for young women in Urban New York, 2005

- Recipient - Outstanding work in Education and Community Service by the New York Chapter of the National Negro Professional and Business Women
- Recipient – Governor's Harriet Tubman Spirit Award, Albany, N. Y., March 2006
- Recipient of the 2007 National Association of ESEA Title I Parents Regional Conference Award for On-Going Support to Parents in Region II
- NYU Invitation to Phi Delta Kappa Membership, 1996
- Sojourner Truth Award National Chapter of the National Negro Professional and Business Women, 2016
- Honored with HCCI building named Dr. Joan O. Dawson Plaza.

Dr. Dawson is the mother of one grown daughter and one grown son. She has one granddaughter and a great-grandson. Her interests include traveling, oil painting, and spending time with family. This book is dedicated to her extremely large family to remind them of the importance of history and heritage.

You can contact her at joan.odawson@nyu.edu

Page Blank Intentionally

Chapter I
Brand New

Daddy drove Mother to New Orleans on that eventful day in October, for that was where most of the African American babies were born and probably most of the White babies also. Charity Hospital was free, and it was the beginning of the Depression in Baton Rouge—all over, in fact. Times were hard, but Daddy reminded Mother that they at least had a roof over their heads, "Annie, we have a house paid for, and we own it. We have food and clothing, and we are doing just fine. Although I don't have a steady job right now, I can fix cars, build things, and I am also a pretty good gardener. I can add another room to the house if we decide that we need it."

Mother was a worrier, however, and his words did little to comfort her. She had grown up off of Perkins Road in a small cabin with her mother and her preacher father. Papa did not own his property as Daddy did. He did not have a car as Daddy did. He did, however, have a wagon and a horse. He used them to haul produce from his garden up and down Perkins Road and to sell fresh vegetables to anyone who would buy from him. He lived with his wife, my grandmother, Mama Harriet. They were now alone in the small cabin setting off Perkins Road. In fact, it was way

off of Perkins Road. The small path that led off of Perkins Road to their cabin was flocked with tall grass and weeds on both sides. As a child, that path seemed at least a half mile off of Perkins Road. The wide car-sized path served as an exit and entrance for us when we were dropped off to visit. It was the entrance and exit for him as he rode in his wagon to Perkins Road to sell his wares.

Papa's children, all six of them, including my mother, were all grown with families of their own, except for one sister, Auntie Margaret, who died before I was born. Coming back to the conversation during the drive to New Orleans, where I was to enter the world, it was intense, "Chester, we have three children to take care of, including this one who is on the way." Mother reminded him as if he didn't already know. "I hope it is a boy," she added with a smile. At that time, the doctors had no way of telling whether a child was a boy or girl before birth.

Mother had begun her labor pains in the middle of the day, but she did the best she could to wait until Daddy came home after his day of part-time work planting flowers and trees in the Manship's yard. I opened my eyes in New Orleans the next day. However, my parents only went there to bring me into this world as I lived and grew up on Essen Lane in Baton Rouge, Louisiana. After that traumatic day of my mother screaming from pain during my delivery and me screaming from the smack they gave me after birth and

Fearless

after the thought of coming into this world, I arrived healthy and with everything in place and in order. Childbirth did not include any kind of anesthesia or other drug to reduce the pain back then, but despite the excruciating pain during my struggle to enter this world, my mother persevered through. However, that smile would likely have been much brighter had I been a boy.

Daddy was elated when he retrieved us after three days. I remember when he opened the blanket and peeked at me, his little reddish black baby girl. Daddy was not allowed to stay with Mother until I made my entrance into the world, so he drove back to Baton Rouge to wait for the call to come and get us. Although I was born the next day, Daddy had to wait a day while they checked me out. So, he waited in the waiting room until Mother and I were ready to go home on the third day. Then, he brought Mother and me home to Baton Rouge. When he peered at me in my new pink outfit and my blanket with pink bears all over it, he had no idea what Mother and I had gone through to come into this world. It was a painful entrance for her and a shocking one for me, but we made it together. I know he thought I was cute with the way he smiled as he folded the blanket back and looked into my eyes for the first time. It was the beginning of a fantastic, loving relationship that would last forever.

My address in Baton Rouge was Route 2, Essen Lane.

In fact, that was the address of all of the families on the approximately three-mile stretch of the "street" called Essen Lane. Various aunts and uncles brought mother soup, food, broth, and other homegrown meals. I was only fed milk, but that was fine. I thrived and had a normal childhood, even during the midst of The Depression. I grew up in what most might call a collectivist sort of culture; I was surrounded by family everywhere. We depended on each other and shared a set of common values and ways of acting and interacting, extending to food, transportation, and goals for adults and children. In fact, it was almost like our whole tribe—if you can call it a tribe—was there to help us kids grow and learn.

Daddy's siblings were Ida, Edna, Griffin, Kernan, Ernest, Edinborough, and John. Uncle John was the firstborn child and the only one who did not live on Essen Lane. He also did not share the same mother as the others but was instead the child of my paternal grandfather's first wife. As I've mentioned before, Essen Lane is about three miles, give or take a half mile, that intersects with Jefferson Highway on one end and with Perkins Road on the other end. Between those two intersections, there are many cross streets, not as prominent as Jefferson Highway or Perkins Road, but very busy with many different types of businesses, doctors' offices, related health care, and other assorted shopping outlets. There is also a railroad track that crosses Essen Lane closer to the Perkins Road

Fearless

intersection.

All Essen Lane residents shared two mailboxes. Our mail came in the box that was located in front of my Uncle Mankey's house, which was three houses down from ours. All Oby and Coleman's mail (the married name of Daddy's sister) went to that single box. Whoever collected the mail also sorted it and delivered it to the rightful owners or just placed it back in the box to be retrieved by the proper recipients.

Our Lady of the Lake Hospital is a major structure that is situated on Essen Lane. Our Lady of the Lake Hospital was originally located downtown in Baton Rouge; however, as Essen Lane changed from rural to metropolitan, the hospital was rebuilt on Essen Lane. The new hospital is a massive building with a manicured lawn, shrubberies, and trees, with an assortment of cosmetic and necessary additions to provide easy access and attractiveness to its facilities and its several entrances. Essen Lane itself is now lined with grocery stores, pharmacies, restaurants, shops, boutiques, a restored Pike Burden Museum, State Office buildings, service stations, and other types of services, stores, and shops. Generally, it is a hustling, bustling thoroughfare.

"By Him therefore let us offer the sacrifice of praise to God continually, that is, the fruit of our lips giving thanks

to His name."

- Hebrews 13:15

Chapter II
Time

How things change! What a difference from the time I entered this world and began my journey of growing up on that same "street" called Essen Lane.

The neighborhood in which my family and I lived was quite different from what it is today. First of all, it was extremely "country"; that's how it was described. *"You live in the country!"* I was told many times by my high school classmates as they laughed. They were right. The road was a rock road. Yes, rocks, not cement or asbestos. The rocks were the kind that you could pick up and throw at something or someone. It was also narrow. There was a ditch that ran the full length of the road in front of all of the houses on Essen Lane.

After a hard rain, of which we had many, we also saw eels swiftly dashing through the clear, sometimes rippling, water in the ditch. I often wondered where they were going in such a hurry and if they had ever stopped to rest. They were so fast and beautiful. There was nothing to compare them with! They appeared to be a beautiful iridescent blue, but they never slowed down for me to really examine their beauty. They traveled so fast through the fresh rainwater that parted as they zipped through it, leaving ripples behind

them, that I never knew where they went, how they lived, and where they were most comfortable. "Where are you going in such a hurry?" I asked them, but they were gone already. They always seemed to be in such a hurry.

Dogs ran loose in the yard and never came in the house; some were friendly and paused for a pat or a piece of bread and a hug. Others barked ferociously as though they were about to attack at any minute, their sharp teeth ready to shred one to bits. Sometimes, yelling a loud "get away" was enough to send them scampering. Other times, it spurred them on. In fact, we were taught to walk with a stick in case one of the dogs was really angry. Cats came in and out. Some lived outside, while others lived inside. Sometimes, they would disappear for days on end but would always return. No litter box or special provisions were made for them; they ate people's food, scraps from the table, or whatever lizards, insects, birds, or other creatures they could catch. They survived and made great companions for me because they seemed to understand me in a way that no one else seemed to. They were furry and felt good on the fingers and face. They did not need me, but I guess I needed them for comfort.

Plumbing only became available on Essen Lane after a few years, and until then, our toilet was outdoors. For those few years, the toilet was a considerable distance from the house, probably because of the smell; however, for me, that

also meant being very conscious of snakes when venturing to the toilet. We had chamber pots for the house at nighttime. My brothers or my mother always "emptied the chamber pot" in the mornings. Eventually, when the city installed water lines, my father installed indoor plumbing, and we had a real bathroom, as did the rest of the families on Essen Lane. I was eight years old at the time.

We still saw snakes all the time. They were in the garden, the weeds, when we picked berries, or anywhere. Seeing a snake or two on the road or crawling out of the ditch in front of the house was nothing out of the ordinary.

There were two canals in our neighborhood: one on Essen Lane and one on Starring Lane, with a bridge over the canals providing passage over both. For us, the bridges also provided access to the canals, where we caught crawfish on a pole with a piece of salt meat tied to the end of a string attached to the pole or sometimes caught other small fish with poles. The canal on Starring Lane also served as the body of water used by the church for baptismal ceremonies.

We also ate lots of fruit off the land growing up. We picked buckets of figs, pears, and pecans. We also picked strawberries, blackberries, and muscadines. Family members made wine, jam, and jelly from the variety of berries we picked in the woods, off the bushes, and the

trees. These woods were in the areas that lined the sides of at least the first family house in the back of all our yards and on the other side of the road in fields and pastures that seemed to be owned by nobody. I later found out that the property across the road belonged to Louisiana State University.

Mother raised vegetables in her garden behind the house. She also raised many animals, including chickens and a cow or two. She also always had a pig or two somewhere in a pig pen behind the house. I loved the land and all of the animals. The pigs, chickens, cats, friendly dogs, turtles, and other creatures, except for snakes and spiders, were all accepted.

My first pet was a pig. I liked two names that I couldn't decide between, so he was sometimes called Wiggly and sometimes Oink. I loved him, and he loved me, too. He followed me through the yard and sometimes into the house—not with Mother's permission, however. His trips inside were clandestine and between me and him. It was our great adventure when no one was looking. I believe I eventually and unintentionally ate him for dinner; however, Mother and Daddy made sure that I did not know Wiggly had become a family meal. I figured out later that I was probably taken for a ride in our car, my favorite activity with Daddy, while Wiggly was being slaughtered. I was not brought back home until the murder had been

Fearless

committed and the evidence prepared for distribution among the family and at our family dinner. I knew that I could not express anger with Daddy even though he orchestrated the murder of Oink. Although he was not the killer, he had to have been one of the culprits who planned the deed. Growing up, children did not openly show anger toward a parent. We were taught to "stay in the place of a child." That meant sucking it up! So, things, attitudes, and situations did not change with me after we ate Wiggly.

Daddy regularly hunted coons, rabbits, squirrels, opossums, and, occasionally, deer. When these animals were killed, Daddy sold the skins to the local furrier in Baton Rouge. He also shot flocks of birds out of the sky and fished; the latter was our main source of food, along with the vegetables from mother's beloved garden, where snap beans, okra, watermelons, cucumbers, squash, tomatoes, butterbeans, and other vegetables grew plentifully.

We were barefoot most of the time, not because we did not have shoes but because it was more comfortable and it was too hot for shoes and socks. Shoes were for Sundays, holidays, and school. My everyday attire included shorts and midriff tops, except on Sundays, holidays, and special school attire. Mother made my dresses for school, and I got newly purchased outfits for Easter and Christmas. Sometimes, I even got a store-bought dress for church.

Joan Oby Dawson

Essen Lane, for us, meant family. Although there were families other than the Obys and Colemans, we were all together, one large village of a family.

My immediate family consisted of my oldest brother, Junior, aka Chester Oby Jr., and my second brother, Buck, who was born Lloyd Lorenzo Oby. Twelve years later, my mother had another baby, Kerney Lee, my youngest brother. I was extremely disappointed that he was not a girl.

The family was proud and strong yet humble and aware of all that was going on around them. My parents anchored and grounded us when we were quite young. They showed love by their actions, without ever using the word "love." This word was rarely used except when a family member was going on a trip.

"Of Joseph, he said: "Blessed of the Lord is his land, with the precious things of heaven, with the dew and the deep lying beneath."

- Deuteronomy 33:13

Chapter III
Love

My best friend growing up was one of my first cousins. Tess was a double first cousin. Our mothers were sisters, and our fathers were brothers. Tess and I spent many afternoons and weekends riding our bicycles up and down Essen Lane and also venturing long distances on Perkins Road. We even rode on the nearby railroad track, enjoying the juggle of the tires crossing each track as we cycled along, thinking nothing of the consequences of an approaching train that might catch us when we were on an elevated section with no place to get off the track if we needed such an exit. Tess and I also played hopscotch, jump rope, jacks, and other games that could be shared by two girls who were as close as possible.

Our "coming of age" venture was a trip to Chicago to stay with Uncle George, our mothers' brother. It was a summer of adventures, movies, and roaming around the streets of Chicago while Uncle George was at work. We were both in our late teens and looking for adventure.

Tess and I remained good friends through the years, including having a double wedding. The wedding was written up on the society page of the local African American newspaper.

Tess was the sister I never had. We ensured that we stayed in touch even though we lived on opposite sides of the country. We shared in family gatherings and conversations or just called to share what was going on in our lives and continue to do so even today. That bond from when we were quite young is still strong.

There was also Yvonne, another first cousin, with whom I shared a different type of friendship than Tess. Yvonne and her younger sister, Joyce Elaine, were the only children of Uncle Mankey, another of Daddy's brothers who lived on the other side of our house. Although Uncle Mankey had another son from an earlier marriage, we did not see him often. Uncle Mankey's real name was Griffin Oby, but all of his nieces and nephews called him Uncle Mankey. He had graduated from Howard University as a student, earning the nickname of "Fess" or, sometimes, Doc (both nicknames referring to having finished college or having taught as a professor). Even though he finished college, he did not pursue a career as a professor. He returned to Baton Rouge, taught mathematics at the high school, and eventually became an elementary school principal. His seven siblings, everyone on Essen Lane, and the surrounding community honored him as an accomplished and educated man.

Uncle Mankey was chosen by the family to be the one to attend college because his complexion was the lightest.

The idea underlying this behavior was that his skin tone would increase his chances of success. Therefore, all the brothers contributed financially so he could complete his college education. Uncle Mankey was the first-generation college graduate in the family.

Auntie Alice, Uncle Mankey's wife, was from Donaldsonville, a quaint little town whose African American residents were mostly fair-skinned Creole people. Auntie Alice was no exception. There were some residents who did not fit the qualifications, but they were few. Most residents tended to be fair-skinned with "silky or soft, curly bordering on kinky" hair. It was then a rural area mostly occupied by Catholics. Auntie Alice was Catholic, and since Uncle Mankey had wanted to marry her, he had converted to Catholicism. Yvonne and Joyce were Catholic and fair-skinned. They had cousins on their mother's side who would come up from Donaldsonville to Baton Rouge to visit on occasional Sundays after church. On those Sundays, I was not allowed to visit Yvonne.

Due to the impact of Jim Crow laws, even among people of color, my mother wanted to make sure no one took advantage of or made fun of me due to my darker skin color. Jim Crow reaffirmed the status of white supremacy through the variety of discrimination and segregation laws it laid down aimed at African Americans in the South. It lasted through the 1960s and represented the most systemic

effort to assert white supremacy after the end of slavery in attempts to curb individual freedoms based on race.

The name Jim Crow was synonymous with discriminatory laws aimed at Black people. Jim Crow was a stock character in minstrel shows, where White performers dressed in rags and blackface to mock Black culture, strengthening bigoted stereotypes for laughs.

Not only did these laws assert the complete dominance of the White folk, but they also served to create division between Blacks—the lighter your skin was, the better you were treated. My mother, I am sure, had experienced that in her life, being the one sister in her family who had a brown complexion. The other two sisters, along with her mother and older brother, were fair in complexion.

"I'm going to play with Yvonne," I announced.

"No, you're not," Mother's stern voice retorted.

"Why not?"

"You're just not going. Now go in the yard and get away from me."

That was it! The matter was settled. All I could do at that point was grumble under my breath—I didn't dare to go against her wishes.

Fearless

Although I was never treated differently from Yvonne or her Creole cousins, when I happened to see them, Mother would not take the chance of it happening. It was a color thing, but I never really thought about it at the time. I thought Mother was being mean. Little did I know she had my best interests at heart.

Our family was an array of skin tones that covered the gamut, so I never focused on color differences. Mother and Daddy never discussed skin color with any of us. We grew up in a family where everyone was accepted, or at least overtly. We did, on frequent occasions, hear Uncle Mankey speak of "his beautiful girls," referring to Yvonne and Joyce. We sort of instinctively knew it was because of the lightness of their skin. Other members of the family were aware, including my mother.

There was also the part religion played in our lives. As opposed to Baptist or Methodist churches, Catholicism was dominated by the fair-skinned and/or Creole members of the community. Uncle Mankey and his family were Catholic, while the rest of the family were Baptist or Methodist. So I thought that maybe it was the Catholic thing.

Although both Yvonne and Tess were close to me in terms of age and association, I had a different type of relationship with each one. The three of us never played

together. For me, it was always one cousin or the other—not a choice but a circumstance. Yvonne and I enjoyed sewing, drawing, cutting out patterns, hair styling, and acting. Both my mother and Auntie Alice had pianos in the houses. Yvonne played the piano at the Catholic Church in Baton Rouge. I liked singing. So many afternoons or Sundays, Yvonne would play the piano at her house or my house, mostly at my house. We sang and enjoyed each other's company, doing each other's hair, sewing clothing, and generally being regular girls.

Yvonne would be playing the piano, accompanying me as I would belt out a favorite blues song:

"Well, I'm goin' upon the mountain

To face the rising sun

If I find anything good

I'm gonna bring my good man some

Cause I'm a hip-shaking mama

And I love to Georgia Bounce so slow

Well, he used to be yours

Aw, but he won't be yours anymore

Anymore, anymore

Fearless

It takes a rockin chair to rock

A rubber ball to bounce

A little bitty baby to get it every ounce

Cause I'm a hip shakin mama

And I love to Georgia Bounce so slow

Well, he used to be yours

But he won't be yours anymore

Anymore"

I loved singing that song, and Yvonne loved banging it out on the piano. That was our favorite, but we had many others—mostly blues songs of the South and a few spirituals, including Amazing Grace.

Yvonne was prematurely gray, so I was tasked with keeping the gray hair from growing on her head. I cut it out on a regular basis. Yvonne and I sewed dresses, styled each other's hair, enjoyed activities that engaged us in projects together and laughed a lot.

"Touch not my anointed and do my prophets no harm."

- Psalm 105:15

Joan Oby Dawson

Chapter IV
Heritage

Growing up, I realized my nature was that of a true and determined introvert. However, looking back, I think I had both introverted and extroverted qualities. I liked making people laugh. However, I also enjoyed being alone in the yard during the day. At night, I resorted to the swing on the front porch. The squeaking of the swing as it swung forward and then backward was a perfect setting for daydreaming, staring at the many stars that dressed the sky and gazing at the amazing images that stood out in the cloud formations. The clouds were fascinating.

As the afternoon flowed into the evening and then night, the changing images and shapes enabled me to travel to distant places, see animals, find the big and little dipper, see kings and queens of Africa, people, and places that I dreamed or sometimes read about. I could not wait to find David and his slingshot or Daniel in the lion's den with the lion sleeping peacefully next to him. Their varied formations took me away to places in a make-believe world that fulfilled all of my dreams. I would do this on a regular basis until my mother would call me inside to prepare for bedtime. My inner thoughts and ideas revealed many things to me and about me. I was meditating without ever being

aware of it.

Daddy held a special place in my heart. "My daddy can do anything," I boldly told anyone who might be listening. Some laughed at me for saying that, but I didn't care. It was the absolute truth. Anyone who denied this fact was not my friend, and I avoided the person who did not see that. One of my earliest memories is from when I was probably a toddler. I remember Daddy often throwing me up into the sky and catching me. It was exhilarating, and I giggled. I totally trusted him, as I did for the rest of his life. Every time I revisit these memories, it fills me with warmth and love for my father. I also remember riding in the car with him. He loved doing things that annoyed my mother when they had an argument.

Among his pastimes, Daddy was a gambler. Mother was happy when he came in and threw a pile of money in the middle of the bed, and they argued when he lost money. Daddy was also a carpenter. He added rooms to our house, built a carport, and he, along with the other brothers, helped relatives build homes. He was also a mechanic. The entire neighborhood brought their cars to him to be repaired. He also taught me a bit about starting a stalling car. My Daddy was a bricklayer, a gardener, having planted beautiful flowering bushes in our yard. Four oak trees presently stand gracefully in front of a restaurant on Essen Lane, where our home once stood. Those trees were planted by my Daddy

when they were only saplings. They can tell this story much better than I can.

Daddy was not only talented with his physical skills but also extremely mentally sharp. He was the person in the family who was sought after whenever there was a dispute, conflict, or challenging issue in the family that needed to be addressed. Whether it was the deed to a piece of property, a disagreement among family or others, or a problem with a salesperson or a business person, Daddy was the one who provided the wisdom for a way out. He was the one who organized and divided the heir property on Essen Lane, assuring that it was equitable and fair among the siblings. With the onset of television, Daddy watched the news and current affairs daily, as well as all of Joe Lewis' fights. He also watched cowboy shows and movies. Daddy was a brilliant man with only a sixth-grade education, which always caused me to wonder about unfulfilled potential among our youth.

Mother and Daddy were less than a century from the Emancipation Proclamation of 1863. They were born in the early 1900s. Louisiana was a tough, racist place, including Baton Rouge. They were less than a generation removed from slavery. They both had experienced discrimination for all of their lives.

Mother taught school in Blanks, Louisiana. Blanks was

across the Mississippi River in Point Coupee Parish. Mother would go over to Blanks on a Sunday night and return on Friday afternoon. Daddy drove her over the Mississippi River on the ferry most of the time since there was no bridge to Blanks or to cross the Mississippi. I still remember the drive down to the entrance of the ferry. The road was muddy, with the Mississippi River trail leading to the ferry... I was always afraid that the car would slip into the Mississippi. It was not a cement road onto the ferry but a muddy path. The car slipped and slid side to side while the tires were spinning to get a grip in the Mississippi River mud all the time, with Daddy maneuvering to make sure that he stayed on the narrow, river-lined path that led to the ferry. Each time we took that trip, I was scared that we would end up in the river. There were cars in front and behind him waiting to approach the ferry. Once on the ferry, the cars lined up in rows, and it slowly crossed the river to repeat this same process of leaving the ferry to go onto the land leading to Highway 190, the narrow two-lane highway that led to Blanks.

Mother was extremely creative. Although her profession was teaching, she sewed, made most of my dresses, and made beautiful quilts by hand, some of which I still have. She crocheted, knitted, and embroidered beautiful things for the house. Items that she did not give to others she used for special occasions at home. Mother was a beautiful woman. I can still see her in the backyard with

her soft, flowing voile dress draped around her body. Sometimes, she wore a laced slip underneath it, and sometimes she didn't. I admired her beauty, her gracefulness, and her charm. On occasion, I was embarrassed by her beauty and the way others stared at her. By and large, she was quiet and strong. Mother was the disciplinarian in the family, and Daddy was the fun one. She had tremendous respect for Daddy, although she pulled the strings. Whenever decisions were made, I would hear, "Go ask your daddy" or "Find out from your daddy."

My maternal grandfather, Papa, was a Baptist preacher when he was not on his wagon selling vegetables up and down Perkins Road, Staring Lane, and Highland Road. His name was James Bickham. Papa was one of the Charter Members of Greater Hollywood Baptist Church, the little church on the corner of Staring Lane and Perkins Road. All the children grew up in that church. We sat on the mourner's bench there for days and hours, were baptized there, went to Sunday school, sang in the choir, and observed the interaction of the members as they went about with all of the church business. The children observed as the preacher, whether Papa or a visiting preacher, preached to a crescendo and would not stop until the women shouted. Usually, after two or three women shouted, the preacher would end his sermon. Mother never shouted—she only cried when preaching was good.

Church was a place for shouting and crying. Mother cried on most occasions, even when not in church. She appeared to wear her feelings on her shoulders. I believe I tend to hide my tears for that reason. Papa's moaning and gyrations and hacks had the church members, especially the women, swaying back and forth. The men mostly sat stoically, shouting a firm "Amen" or "Yes, Lord," or just "Preach!!!"

Church was a place for worshiping and also for socializing. Mother and all other women in the church wore hats and dressed as elegantly as they could afford. My mother wore suits and, sometimes, gloves. The girls wore dresses, no pants, and the boys wore suits, no matter how young. Although the pants may be short, due to the climate, a jacket was always a part of the attire of the younger boys.

Church crying was different from funeral crying. Funerals were special occasions at Greater Hollywood. There was always food, lots of tears, and after the body was buried, some laughter. The children always wore white, and the women wore black. No one wore bright colors. That was totally inappropriate.

Aunt Dot was married to another one of Daddy's brothers. She was the biggest shouter at the church. Ms. Laura was not a blood aunt but definitely considered a member of the family. She was a big woman who jumped

around like a chicken with its head off when she shouted. When she began swaying back and forth, we knew to get out of her way because she was going to thrust her hands back behind her with her arms out in full swing, and somebody might get hit. She then got up and jumped up and down, getting stiff and rigid, before she fell backward. The children thought it all very funny but did not dare laugh out loud.

We performed the Easter program, the Christmas program, and the Children's Day performance. The Children's Day performance was a performance to raise a small amount of money for whatever the cause might be. It was probably to pay Papa. The secretary's report, read out loud from the back of the church, would lay out the amount collected during the service. Thirty-five to fifty dollars was a good collection for a regular church day.

Papa was strict; his preaching was robust. I was around 12 years old when he died. When he was in bed, sick, all of the children were called into the room where he lay so that he could say goodbye to them. That's when I realized that he was a gentle and caring man. He lay there, holding our small hands one at a time, looking at us and not saying much. A slight tear in one of his eyes spoke of his love for us and maybe his hope for our future.

My maternal grandmother, Harriet Murdock, was a

quiet, small, fair-skinned lady who was always busy. From sweeping the small cabin of a house to cooking on the wood-burning stove, she was always doing one thing or another. We called her "Mama." She was a fair-skinned little lady who lived in a three-room cabin with a wooden front window and a huge mulberry tree in the front yard. The cabin was much like the slave quarters depicted at the Whitney Plantation Museum, located between Baton Rouge and New Orleans. Both Mama and my mother swept their yards. The yard on Perkins Road and the yard on Essen Lane was always clean. We had no need to be concerned about stepping on a rock or broken glass that might hurt our feet. Much later, I learned it to be an African tradition. I also kept up the tradition before moving to New York City, where yards were nothing like the clean, sprawling yards in Baton Rouge. Both paternal grandparents died before I was born.

***

"Get in the car, we're going out," Mother told us. My brothers Buck, Junior, and I gathered ourselves up and went to Daddy's Chevrolet. They were going out on their Friday night outing to the movies and then to get fried fish or chicken. Bernard's, a Baton Rouge family-owned restaurant, was known for fried chicken. There were only two places in Baton Rouge where Black people could get takeout food. One of them was Bernard's, and the other

Fearless

was Delpit's family-style restaurant. The Delpits were a Creole family in Baton Rouge. It was either one of the two for Mother and Daddy. Mother and Daddy usually went to a movie at The Temple Theater, the movie house for African Americans. They would see a cowboy movie and then go to Bernard's for chicken or Delpit's for chicken or fish. We would be dropped off on Perkins Road, where the narrow grassy lane led to that cabin in the woods where Mama and Papa would be waiting for us. Sometimes, we spent the night. Other times, they picked us up after and took us home. When they picked us up, we delighted in the chicken or fish they had saved for us and that we ate in the back seat of the car.

When we spent the night at Mama's, we played together in the yard. In the morning, we climbed that big mulberry tree to pick the biggest and juiciest fruit, picking and eating fresh off the tree. Early in the morning, we would go and get those mulberries; otherwise, the birds would get to them. There were no snakes in that tree, but there were snakes everywhere else.

On one occasion, when Mother and Daddy let us out on Perkins Road to run up the path, we were greeted by a king snake standing at the edge of the grass waiting for us. My brothers made a run for the house, leaving me a bit behind. My brothers were faster and just dashed off, leaving me to try to catch up. The snake caught up with us,

passed us, and disappeared in the off-shoot of grass on the side of the trail. It was the first time I saw a snake stand up on its tail before chasing us down the trail.

"You have set your glory in the heavens. Through the praise of children and infants, you have established a stronghold against your enemies."

- Psalms 8

Chapter V
Dirt

My favorite spot to play in the backyard was under a large oak tree. I was drawn by nature and loved the fresh rain-made mud after a thunderstorm. I also played in the clovers that grew in the front yard. I loved being by Daddy's side as he fascinated me with his planting or caring for the flowering bushes, the camellias, the azalea, the crape myrtles, or other flowering plants or trees. The oaks he had planted as small saplings now seemed to need no caring. They had grown enormous, independent, strong, and long-lasting. Because of Daddy, there were large oak trees shadowing both sides of our home. Those trees now overshadowed a restaurant. Playing in the mud, under those trees, was my favorite thing to do. I absolutely loved running around in the rain.

Mother was one of those traditional women who thought that girls and boys should be kept separated at least most of the time or unless an adult was present. This rule did not include my brothers, who were my protectors. We were siblings and were always together, except when they were doing outdoor chores or away on some project with Daddy. They had a bit more freedom than I did. I was handed the indoor chores, or at least a few of them, if not

all. Washing dishes was the one I did on a regular basis. Ironing pillowcases and shirts was another, and it was the one I hated the most. My brothers' chores seemed fun as they included trimming the hedges in the yard, going on errands, cutting the yard, and other outdoor activities. However, most of the time, my brothers were also handed the duty of being in charge and caring for me. There was definitely a difference in how we were treated based on our gender. I didn't recognize it at the time, but it felt wrong. I was mainly a lone ranger until I hit my teenage years.

My cousin Tess had a younger sister, "Red." Her real name was Harriet, named after our grandmother. Sometimes, Red came over with Tess. Later, Auntie Etta had another girl whom she named Violet. However, she was lovingly called "Pug."

Auntie Etta came to visit Mother almost daily, only occasionally missing a day in the week. Tess and I were together then, along with the times we pulled out our bikes for adventures "on the road."

Tess and I played together constantly, ignoring both Red and Pug. Pug seemed to quickly grow into this cute little sassy girl who was able to have her way much more than when we did at her age. We were approaching our teenage years when she was born. As we grew older, Red seemed to grow into our circle of interests. Pug also did as

she became older, and age was no longer a factor for young adults.

Though I did not have one myself, I understood the bond between sisters, thanks to my cousins. I could observe the closeness and togetherness that my cousins and siblings shared naturally. Mother and Auntie Etta shared that natural bond. They saw each other almost daily. I never understood why Auntie Etta almost always left Mother crying after a visit. Auntie Etta would storm out of the house after a visit and walk down the lane to her house four doors away, leaving Mother upset and crying almost uncontrollably. "Why are you crying, Mother?" I wanted to know. I was never told, nor was I privy to the conversations that caused Mother to cry after a visit from her only sister, who lived close to her. Mother's other sisters were Aunt Margaret and Aunt Ethel. Aunt Margaret died before I was born, and Aunt Ethel lived in Chicago.

As Mother grew in age, she continued to work tirelessly. She cried when she could no longer teach, but determined not to be a stay-at-home woman; she started nursing. She took a course, got a certificate as a practical nurse, and started an entirely new career. However, she was growing older and more prone to illness. Her health eventually caused her to stop working when she was about 80 years of age. After a few years of being cared for by Buck, my brother, she agreed to come to New York and

live with me. My Daddy had died six years earlier. Mother was with me in New York when she died.

> *"Praise be to God and Father of our Lord Jesus Christ, the father of compassion and the God of all comfort, who comforts us in all our troubles with the comfort we ourselves receive from God."*
>
> — 2 Corinthians 3:5

Chapter VI
Qualified

My university experiences included my undergraduate life at an HBCU, Southern University, and my pursuit of a Master's Degree at the newly integrated Louisiana State University. In addition to that, I spent a summer at Stanford University and New York University, which, to me, was justified travel.

All these experiences, for different reasons, impacted my decisions in life and helped me chart a course that brought me to where I am today. People now question whether education is still the gateway to success, and I know that many people are highly successful without degrees. However, a degree does not inhibit other pursuits; it only enhances them.

After graduating from Southern University and working for a few years, I returned to it to take more courses. I enjoyed school. It was easy for me, so I wanted more. LSU was in the early stages of integration at the time. My professor, Dr. Sam, said, "What are you doing here at Southern? Go to LSU." Being obedient to an influential man, I immediately went to LSU. I registered as the first Black student in the Department of Communication Sciences and Disorders, as it is now named. I had no idea of what I was doing or the

consequences, nor did I give the idea too much thought before acting. I had never been to the LSU campus before, although we did not live far from the campus.

Although LSU was in the beginning stages of integration, after the Brown v. Board of Education decision, the department I enrolled in had not yet been integrated. I was also the first African American to pursue a Master of Science Degree in Speech Pathology and Audiology from LSU. My life was in the hands of that department because I was a vessel void of direction. I was terrified.

Fortunately, despite the boycotts, the system of racism, and the subtle and overt racism, I was greeted by Dr. Wise, the department head, with empathy and perspective. My fear and innocence were glaring because I did not know how to conceal them. I was naïve and had given no thought to my actions. It was a good move. I was a trailblazer without even realizing it. As I looked back later, I was also an open book to Dr. Wise.

Professor Wise opened his office and his kindness to me. He told me to come to him if I experienced any discomfort. He saw the insecurity and uncertainty of a 21-year-old woman venturing into the center of a racist society to pursue a degree in a department as the first African American – other departments at LSU were integrated, but

not yet this one. I believe he saw the potential and knew that integration with LSU was inevitable.

For me, the entire experience was one of guarded optimism. I never felt truly comfortable in classes. The subject matter was easy, so I did my work, left, and came back the next day. It could have been a terrible experience, but Dr. Wise made it a "safe" one. He made me feel that he cared about my progress and me as a person. He also peeked into my classes on a regular basis to ensure all was going well.

Dr. Wise was concerned with my needs as opposed to the needs of the previously segregated department, where I was suddenly a student who comfortably disappeared into a sea of White students. There were other challenges facing me at LSU. To get a Master's degree in Speech Pathology and Audiology, 300 supervised clock hours were required. These clock hours are usually gained by working in the clinic. The clinic at LSU was not yet integrated; this had to change.

Dr. Wise, the Chair of the Department, met with me to work out a solution. Since I was not allowed to work in the clinic due to the presence of White parents and children, I was given a period of time to work in the clinic without the company of White parents and children from the community. The second phase of the solution was that I

had to go into the community of the African American world and solicit clients. This meant knocking on doors and trying in any other way to find children who had communication problems. I had to then arrange to get them to the University when the clinic was closed and work with them during those hours. It was a cumbersome process, but it was the only solution available for me to meet the requirements to fulfill the needed 300 clock hours. Somehow, I fulfilled the requirement. Somewhere during that process, I was eventually allowed to see my clients during the regular clinic hours with White parents and children. Fortunately, there were no incidents.

Although I had to recruit my own African American students from the communities, I was required to work with them in the clinic. Dr. Shaver, my drama professor, also required that I break another barrier. The students in his class were required to write a play and act in one of the community productions. That worked well. I played the part of an elf, wearing a costume and, of course, acting like one. So, my race and ethnicity were not revealed to the audience of mostly White people, except for my husband, who was seated in the audience to provide the needed support.

I focus on this graduate school experience more because it was an early lesson in leadership that has served my entire life in how I deal with and relate to others. I did

not become bitter as some other contemporaries have expressed about being the first to integrate. Without my knowledge, Dr. Wise was willing to change a system to show me that he cared. My graduation requirements necessitated that he make changes in the system. This could have been – or maybe was – difficult, but he did it. The White families, some racist, had to learn that this young Black woman would be in the segregated clinic with them and with Black children and Black parents.

    I am sure that Dr. Wise made sacrifices to open those doors for me. He did this without my being even slightly aware of what was happening until I reflected upon the experience much later in life. I learned that one must always be mindful of the needs of the individual as opposed to the organization. Organizations can and sometimes should change, as in the Brown v. Board decision case, which was a tremendous impetus for change across the country. Organizational change can foster individual needs.

I had already experienced two years of teaching before attending LSU. My first job as a teacher of English and drama came easy. During the '50s, schools recruited teachers by visiting college campuses. I was recruited for my first teaching position at Franklinton, Louisiana. Teaching for me was another natural extension of my experiences. The patterns of life included going to college, riding the school bus, coming home after school every day,

and then teaching. All this seemed natural and another step in "life" as usual for a Black girl in the Oby family.

Besides, all of my cousins were teachers. It was the career chosen for the Oby family, given that it was one of the few career paths open for African Americans in the segregated city of Baton Rouge. Southern had a law school, but African Americans interested in medicine had to go to Meharry Medical School or Howard. Teaching, nursing, or maybe a career in a new or scarce field, such as medicine or law, were the only things available for African Americans.

Teaching was easy. The students loved my youth, energy, and knowledge. However, I was at Washington Parish High School for only a year. It was my first experience of being on my own, the first year of teaching, the first year of mentoring and changing the lives of others, the first year of having my own money, the first year of dating, and the year I got married. I turned 20 in October of that year and married in December of the same year. It was a wonderful year for me.

The following year, I took a position where I was teaching English and Drama at Chaneyville High School in Zachery, Louisiana. However, I was fired that year because I had the nerve to get pregnant. Teachers were not allowed to be seen pregnant in front of the high school students

Fearless

back then – even if they were securely married.

My lesson was, "Inequities are to overcome."

"In the world you shall have tribulation: but be of good cheer; I have overcome the world. These things I have spoken to you that in Me you may have peace."

- John 16:33

Chapter VII
Influence

Many people motivated me during my three short years of college at Southern University, including Dr. Sam Brown, my first instructor in the field of speech pathology and audiology, and Dr. Henry, who not only mentored me but also became a lasting friend. More than any other professor, Dr. Henry influenced my future ventures, both in college and graduate school. Our relationship blossomed into a full-time close friendship with him and his wife, Doveal. Dr. Henry took great pride in reminding me that he was an instructor to me and my mother at Southern when she later pursued her bachelor's degree at Southern University.

College life at Southern University was tremendously rewarding. I pledged with Delta Sigma Theta, formed friendships, and became passionate about forming a bowling team of five friends. Bowling and friendships continued after college. The love of acting with the Riverbend Players also only grew in time. C. Van Jordan, the head of the Riverbend Players, and later his replacement, Dr. Carmichael, took what I thought was a particular interest in me – it was probably all the students, but at the time, I thought it was only me. I was able to

participate in all of these things and still managed to always get home back to Essen Lane by 5:00 or 6:00 in the evening. Because of my love for acting, I finally convinced my mother that living on campus would be a good thing. However, upon investigation, I discovered that the dorms were all full. Somehow, my mother knew about an elderly couple who rented to students. They lived close to the campus entrance. I was allowed to stay with this couple. It lasted a short while, less than a semester, until Mother found out that I was getting home around 1:00 in the morning. She did not understand that acting required practice, especially when preparing for a performance.

All of the extracurricular activities influenced my sense of direction. I integrated a bowling alley in Baton Rouge with friends from college who bowled. I also took courses in acting. Later in life, I continued to explore that hobby. I have had the opportunity to be an extra in several movies in New York.

Thank God, some things have changed. However, much is still the same and needs to change.

"My son, forget not my law, but let thine heart keep my commandments for length of days and long life, and peace shall they add to thee."

- Proverbs 3

Joan Oby Dawson

Chapter VIII
Innocence

Highland Road was the main road that ran straight through Louisiana State University from the south of Baton Rouge to the north toward New Orleans. The populations on Highland Road ran the gamut, from the wealthy to the poor, African American, White, Native American, and a sparse number of other cultures. The scenery slowly and distinctly changed as one moved from north of Highland Road through Louisiana State University Campus into South Baton Rouge, a community of African American middle and lower-income residents.

However, going north on Highland Road, the contrast was enormous. The community north consisted of plantation-like homes situated on large lawns, some with small cabins on the property, where African American families still lived on the properties. Others embraced long driveways that led into well-cultivated lawns and garden-like entrances to the homes. There were a few streets that were off shouts of Highland Road that led into private housing. Some of the LSU professors lived in these homes. The LSU community was certainly a stark reminder of the inequities of the two worlds that were so glaring and obvious to the curious.

Joan Oby Dawson

I grew up in the shadow of Louisiana State University, north of both communities. Essen Lane, about two miles from Highland Road, was my cushion. My family, almost the entire family, and an instilled faith were my cushion.

Built in that invisible yet very visible structure of inequality, I know that family plays a key role in understanding and conquering such elements of strangulation.

The first semester of my life at LSU was a period of adjustment. I was 20 years old, inexperienced, and new to White people. Or maybe I should say that they were new to me. I had no friends, acquaintances, or memorable moments that stood out. My life was all about going to school, returning home to my husband, and going to work. At some point, I discovered I was pregnant with my first child. My husband and I were working on several personal projects at the time, one of which was to have a home built in the newly developing Mayfair Park subdivision. Due to work and other commitments, I continued school only by attending summer and evening classes. It took several years for me to complete my degree because of working part-time.

After what seemed like an eternity – probably two or three semesters – Lois, another African American woman from Southern University, enrolled at LSU in the same

department. *"Company at last,"* I thought. Lois and I became friends and remained so well into adulthood and old age. Lois helped me recognize racism in a way that I did not see. One of our professors, an audiology professor, taught us both, but at different times. I had never thought of his many short and curt remarks to me as racist; Lois did.

"You can't see the blue on your blouse. It looks just like skin," the professor commented once while I was pregnant. I was wearing a smart, white blouse over my growing belly and had gotten ink spots on it during class.

"Oh, my God, what have I done?" I stated while trying to wipe the ink stains off.

My audiology professor made other remarks during class, always seeming to point me out. "You may not be able to understand this concept. It may go over your head." I was always baffled and presumed that he did not mean his statements in a harmful way. During my time at LSU, that was the only class in which I got a D.

Overall, my experience at LSU was uneventful. Dr. Wise, the head of the Department, even invited me to his home when he had a gathering of his friends. My husband and I went. Dr. Wise did everything possible to help me adjust. Isolation for any reason goes against the DNA of anyone, especially the young and vulnerable, such as we find in our schools across the country.

Joan Oby Dawson

"In all your ways acknowledge Him, and He will direct your path."

- Proverbs 3:6

Chapter IX
Chances

Paul, my husband, and I met in the spring of my last year of college at Southern University in 1954. I guess you could call our relationship a whirlwind. A few months after meeting, we decided to get married, and so, on December 22, 1954, we tied the knot. We had a beautiful double wedding that included my first cousin, Tess, and her fiancée, Roy. Paul and I were instantly attracted when we met at his sister's house in the early summer of 1954. His sister, Mary Frances, married my first cousin, Angus Oby. We were pretty mixed up as far as marriages go. However, it was typical of the Baton Rouge culture.

Mary Frances lived on Terrace Street in the middle of South Baton Rouge, a direct bus route to Southern University. During my college years, before meeting Paul, Mary Frances' house was a frequent stop for me, both going and coming from Southern University. It seemed only natural that one of the times, I clashed with my mother. I decided to leave home but had no place to go. I ended up at Mary Frances' house, where I stayed for about a week until Mother and Daddy came and fetched me back home. By then, however, Paul had come from the Army, a year older than me, handsome and alluring, and

immediately attracted my attention. I drew him in, too. Mary Frances noticed the sparks and sent him to stay with his mother. So he went to his mother's house, literally around the corner, to stay. That was the beginning of our story.

As our courtship developed, with my new position as a teacher in Franklinton, near New Orleans, he drove me to and from Franklinton, where I resided in a teacher's cottage from Monday to Friday to teach at Washington Parish High School. Our decision to get married was not a romantic one. In reality, we decided to see if we could join Tess and Roy in their marriage, and they agreed. We decided that around October 1954.

Neither of us knew much about marriage. We had no counseling or training; we were only attracted to each other, which grew into love and desire to be together. We enjoyed each other's company and the idea of marriage. I did not know how to cook or do anything expected of a wife. We lived with Paul's mother after the marriage. We continued our lives by going out, doing things together, playing games, attending house parties, playing cards, and generally interacting with friends on weekends. His friends became my friends, and mine became his. The relationship was pretty perfect. Paul landed a job at the Post Office, and I continued teaching. After two years, I got pregnant without ever using birth control. We welcomed our little

girl, whom he absolutely adored, and then two years later, our little boy followed, also with no planning. We loved our children. I engaged the children in church activities, play, school activities, and community play. Paul went fishing and hunting with my father and others in his circle, and our lives continued as an average, young, striving couple in Baton Rouge.

We eventually accomplished our goal and had a house built in Mayfair Park, a newly developing subdivision where middle-class young African Americans were settling. We all knew each other and worked together. Teachers, doctors, lawyers, contractors, mail carriers, college professors, and other like-minded people formed a community based on Christian, church-going principles and values. We supported each other, depended upon each other, and shared common visions and values.

We enjoyed our home and planted two trees together in the front yard. They are now huge oaks, growing together into what is now one giant tree. Those two trees represented us as we grew. In the front yard, we dedicated those trees to ourselves, pledging our love and lives as a couple who grew into each other. Life seemed to be perfect, but little did I know that after only eight years and ten months of being together, Paul would leave me.

Paul went to a football game and did not return, having

run off the road into a huge telegraph pole on the side of the road. That night was truly a nightmare for me. My doorbell rang in the middle of the night. I went to the door to answer it, thinking it was Paul and maybe he could not find his key. I yelled, "The children are sleeping. I'm coming!" When I answered the door, I saw my father on the other end. He and a friend of my husband's greeted me with the news of Paul having been in an accident. I quickly responded, "Let's get to the hospital." I don't remember the words they said to let me know that he had died; I just remember screaming and running outside.

My life was thrust into a totally different direction, and it seemed I had no control over it. However, after some time, I took control for the first time in my life. I realized that I was angry that he had left. I felt that he betrayed me, and I was furious. It took years for me to move on, but eventually, I think I did. I decided to travel, although it was just a notion at the time.

My husband died on October 5th, 1963, just short of nine years of marriage. He was instantly killed when his car ran off the road on Perkins Road into an electric pole. On the impact of the car hitting the light pole, all the lights went out in the neighborhood, including our house. Following Paul's funeral, my house was filled with people, food, flowers, and drinks from neighbors, friends, and family. The funeral and burial all seemed an unending

nightmare. I was devastated to no longer have a partner and to have to feel something so unpleasant up close. I remember the funeral as a bad, horrible dream. Daddy held my arm as I walked into the church to see my husband stretched out in a casket. I did not recognize him and declared in front of everyone that it was not him in the casket. I don't remember much else. I remember my nephew, Michael, telling my son, Paul, "You can share our daddy." That was not the way it was supposed to be.

After Paul's passing, my mother pressured me to move back home, but I did not give up. "I will go home for a while, but I want to live in my own house," I told her. After all, it was the house Paul and I had so lovingly built together. It was home. My stubbornness would not allow me to admit that going home with my mother was exactly what I needed at the time. I was ill-equipped to deal with the death of my husband, the comforting of my children, and the daily picking up of life and moving on. The tears seemed never-ending, and I never seemed to stop crying. I neglected my children and could have been adequately described as a "basket case." It was too bad that someone could not see that I needed help during the early 60s. No one did, and I went on with the unending grief that had attached itself to me as a shield. Somehow, I did move on with life, and so did my children.

Eventually, I returned to work, picking up where I left

off, but things had changed. Neighbors and former friends seemed to be supportive initially, but it became weird as time went by. I was no longer a fit with the couples as before. I started getting calls from men who knew or worked with my husband or neighbors who hunted or fished with Paul. It started with an innocent call to see how I was doing or if there was anything they could do for me, but then escalated to the point that I might need company or be lonely.

It was also challenging to get a legitimate date; I wasn't ready to date anyway. My friends had decided that I was a threat to their marriages. It was the culture of the South. I felt extremely vulnerable. All of this may have been in my head; I had no way of knowing. At that time, as I said, I probably needed counseling. However, that was not the way of a young southern African American woman. That would have been an additional stigma. I would have been labeled "crazy" and, who knows, maybe sent away for treatment – the wrong kind. I continued bowling, a sport I enjoyed, and traveling was added to my list since I now had money.

I decided to travel and see some places and the things I had dreamed of as a little girl sitting in the swing on the front porch of Essen Lane. My purpose was becoming more focused. My first trip was to New York for the Easter weekend. After a beautiful touristy weekend in New York,

Fearless

I returned to pick up where I left off. Mother and Daddy tremendously supported me and my two children, keeping them whenever I decided to take off on some adventure, even if it was just a weekend trip to New York. Life was taking shape, and I was enjoying it!

The trip, although short, was a relief from the overt racism that was engrained in the culture of Baton Rouge. The teachers were segregated, the schools were segregated, and the bathrooms were segregated. The lunch counters at places like Walgreens and other chain stores were segregated. There were Black and White drinking fountains, and eventually, separate bathrooms were established after having no bathrooms for African Americans. There was even a floor in the hospital designated for African Americans; the other floors were for White patients. I must clarify that all of this was taken for granted. Its impact was subtle, but its consequences were great.

One month before the death of my husband, the family was impacted by the 16th Street Church bombing, where one of the four little girls who perished was my husband, Paul's cousin. On September 15th, while in the church to participate in a Sunday adult service, Denise McNair, 11 years old, was one of the victims of the bombing. Although we did not attend the services, my children and I spent Christmas in Birmingham at the home of Peaches and

Joan Oby Dawson

Holmes Hughes, grandparents of Denise. Denise's parents, Maxine and Chris McNair, Peaches, Holmes Hughes, along with me and my two children, all spent Christmas dinner during this gloomy Christmas season in December 1963.

President Kennedy had been assassinated in November, the month after the death of my husband. The whole country was mourning.

In the middle of all of the world's turmoil and my personal upheaval, I reported to work, dropped my children off at school, picked them up after work, and went home.

After a year of working as an itinerant speech pathologist, I was asked by my supervisor to take on the role of a "helping teacher." This role involved staff training and helping teachers with classroom management and effective teaching. Teachers did not wear jeans or go to work looking sloppily; instead, we wore high-heeled shoes and designer dresses. We used frilly umbrellas when it rained and when the sun was bright. We were examples for our students. I was an example for teachers and supervisors as a "helping teacher," a position of status, leadership, and influence that followed my work as a speech pathologist. A major focus of that leadership included how one's attire influences impressions, actions, and results.

"Therefore my brotheren dearly beloved and longed for, my joy and crown, so stand fast in the Lord my dearly

Fearless

beloved, I beseech you."

- Philippians 4

Joan Oby Dawson

Chapter X
Changes

Death is an unnatural phenomenon. When my husband died in a tragic automobile accident, it was a huge, devastating shock. It wasn't just because he was 30 when this happened but also because one can never accept death, even if it comes to someone who is seriously ill. *"Oh, well, the Lord took him."* No, we serve a God of Love. I am sure of it because I believe that somewhere in the Bible, He is called Love, "I am Love." He received him, but He did not take him. All of my Christianity did not help me to understand what had just happened in my life.

Nonetheless, my experience was devastating indeed. It set forth a series of responses that were a direct result of the unnaturalness of death. My experiences in dealing with the shock, the suddenness, and the trajectory of being shot off into an unknown place never seemed to move me forward. Friends and family were there for me.

This was a time in my life when I was struggling between dependence and independence. I had always sought independence from what I saw as impositions from my family. I had gained some semblance of independence through marriage; however, I then found myself in limbo between my parents and my widowhood. I needed my

parents. They were there. I realized that support through surrogacy or good friendship can go a long way in the provision of much-needed stability and sustainment.

Of course, I also had to think of my children who were left without a father. Shocking. I was not in a state to be the kind of mother they needed. I was devastated to the extent that I could not stop crying. My children and I moved back to my parents' house immediately after. There, my mother waited on me, hand and foot.

I was fed breakfast, snacks, and dinner, much of which I did not eat. I took grieving to several levels higher than it had ever been. Friends visited, but finally, as time passed, the visits dwindled. After several months, I finally started going places with a couple of friends who remained loyal. Ann Richardson and her husband, as well as Lois Sam and her husband, were there for me. They took me to places I had gone before and refused to let me withdraw from activities I had done before. I accompanied them to ball games, concerts, and a few house parties that they had at their residence. I returned to work as a speech pathologist in the East Baton Rouge Parish schools and finished my Master's degree at Louisiana State University.

I began bowling again with the same group of women friends whom I had before. I continued to act with the community players, a theatre group started by Margarete

Bayham, a former drama teacher from McKinley High School and my high school Alma Mater. However, everything was meaningless. It was difficult for me to "feel" again. I cried a lot, but only when I was alone. I don't remember doing much with my children except for things that involved my large extended family. We played cards in Auntie Alice's backyard. We laughed a lot. The game was always Bonanza. It was a board game that took its players through several stages of various card games. Polka, spades, keno, twenty-one, and several other games were included. At any stage, one could either win or lose money. I believe we played with pennies and nickels. On a vibrant afternoon, we used quarters. The game was always accompanied by pea pickers, a drink made of frozen lime juice, lots of fruit, and lots of vodka. My cousin Betty, who loved cooking, would concoct and serve the drink to all my cousins, aunts, and other relatives who played.

There were enough cousins around that Paul and Tandra were never alone. As all children, they participated in anything that involved the family except, of course, the drinking. I assumed they got back into the groove of being children in the village that was doing its job of raising them. Of course, we went to church on Sundays and other days when there were church activities. The church played a central role in everything else that went on in the family, although we consisted of Baptist, Catholic, and Methodist churchgoers.

Fearless

Essen Lane was not frequented by cars on a regular basis. It was a rock road. Maybe a car would come through every 10-15 minutes. During one of our intense Bonanza games, and in the middle of sipping pea pickers, we did not notice that there were more cars on the road than usual. Auntie Alice peeked her head out to the back door and yelled. "Why don't somebody see what's going on over the road? The cars are blowing horns."

"What's happening?" Yvonne said as the game continued. Paul and Michael were toddlers at the time and were able to somehow get an old cart, the kind that is at grocery stores today.

"What could be happening?" Betty yelled out. She was always the one who exaggerated everything, so we paid her no attention, continuing our game.

My Auntie Alice poked her head out of her back door and, about ten minutes later, said again, "Somebody go out and see what is going on." Yvonne got up from the card table, moved to the front yard, and yelled, "Agnes, Paul, and Michael are in the road holding up traffic."

We all moved to the front to see my son, Paul (Binky), my son, and Michael, my nephew, both a little more than three years old, pushing the grocery basket in the road with a line of cars behind them, blowing horns frantically. The road was not wide enough for the cars to go around them.

Besides, a fence was on one side of the road and a deep ditch on the other. Of course, we retrieved them and went back to our game. Today, both Annette, Michael's mom, and I would have been brought up on child neglect and maybe would have lost our children. How have the times changed? They grew up normal despite that experience. Paul is an engineer, and Michael is a college professor.

"Trust in the Lord with all your heart, and do not lean on your own understanding. In all your ways, acknowledge him, and he will make straight your paths."

- Isaiah 26:4

Chapter XI
Family

Due to the network of family and other like-minded African Americans, life and personally instilled values on Essen Lane continued to reap a rich harvest. The Oby family continued to broaden its influence and increase in stature. It was a way of life established by ancestors much earlier. We were respected and accomplished. We always owned property. Most of the children finished college. Many were first-generation college graduates holding positions at Southern University as auditors, bursars, and registrars. Some were teachers, nurses, doctors, dentists, and attorneys. Some worked in the Governor's mansion or other public service positions. Some had private positions for companies such as the oil refinery. Some continued as bricklayers, carpenters, electricians, plumbers, or other skills. For the most part, all seemed to have excellent work ethics. They reported to work in their cars, they dressed up well on proper occasions. All in all, they were upstanding middle-class citizens who contributed to the Baton Rouge community in various capacities.

Of course, as in any family, there were a few stragglers – a couple of cousins who broke the law and got into trouble, lived off family, or practiced some other

unacceptable behavior. However, even those who exhibited such behaviors were not outcasts; they were loved and cared for by family.

Frequent family gatherings brought the family together quite regularly. These gatherings included Christmas, Thanksgiving, Easter, and general family picnics. In fact, the strong Christian backgrounds, whether Catholic, Baptist, or Methodist, were firmly in place. Family members were also talented in the arts. Musicians, singers, players of various instruments, and other forms of artistic expression were represented among the entire family.

The Oby family held a secure position in the community. The high value placed on education, including college, cemented the fact that children would never experience hunger or lack of housing.

We began as owners of small homes, some of which were built and expanded by family members. It was inherited property. Our grandparents were smart enough to leave a firm legacy. It was a segregated system, but the children were protected and mostly socialized with each other.

Within the middle of this cushion of middle-class life, I felt a need to move on when I resigned myself as a single parent. So I planned to leave home. Had I known, maybe I would have had second thoughts, but not second moves.

Fearless

My determination and probably stubbornness would not allow me to reconsider.

When I left Louisiana, in the middle of tears streaming down my mother's face, on that balmy morning in June 1968 to visit New York, with the possibility of moving there, I had no idea of what lay ahead, except a temporary relief from the feeling of despair at the loss of my stability. At that young age, not much thought was given to possible consequences. One thing was certain: I did not want to be too far from my parents in case I needed to return quickly.

Before I left, my Uncle Kernan came over to give me a very useful piece of advice, "Aggie, I have one thing to tell you: ***Be what you is, 'cause you can't be what you ain't.***"

I never forgot about it. That piece of advice became a mantra for my life in New York. In fact, Cinni, one of the many artists in the family, designed a magnet with the exact words as stated and spelled. It is on my refrigerator as a reminder always.

My life until then was routine. The culture and the times dictated that an African-American born in Baton Rouge and raised during the 1940s and '50s was destined to be a teacher, a nurse, or, in the case of a man, a teacher, doctor, lawyer, contractor, builder, or a laborer in that field of work. I chose to teach Speech Pathology. It was something different and novel in Baton Rouge. I liked

challenges, so I chose it as my major at Southern University. I did not really think about what I liked or didn't like about teaching, but it was my career path, like it or not. It ended up being a great fit for me. I loved teaching middle and high school youth. My secret dream career was to be an actor. As a child, I loved standing on my head or falling on the floor in front of my family, making them think I had passed out. I liked the drama. I still do. I cannot stand on my head anymore, but I can still act.

Although there were many twists and turns, some form of education became the centerpiece of my existence. As time moved me into other stages of life, I found that I liked real estate, buildings, and especially watching my bank account increase in numbers. As I explored these new horizons, first in California, and then New York, I realized that I needed to be comfortable within my own skin to find my way. Even in New York, where I finally decided to live, it was important to realize that I matter. My growth had to take place within.

Even while working in education, I met the Edwards Sisters Real Estate company and, through one of the realtors, was able to learn about real estate. I was already working with parents throughout my career as an educator, so it was easy to see the missing connection between housing and education. The children were caught in the middle of sometimes very poor communities and

educational expectations. Most of the children of affluent or middle-class parents went to private schools. For the most part, our schools for our children were run by our relatives or close acquaintances. So they were safe.

> *"I can do all things through Christ who strengthens me."*
>
> - Philippians 4:13

Joan Oby Dawson

Chapter XII
Courage

I wanted a house in New York. Once I started my quest, I ended up owning several houses and apartments in New York, all at different times (only one at a time). My first New York ownership was in New Rochelle. I lived there for three years and sold that property to move back to Manhattan. The next one was a brownstone on West 95th Street. Before living there, I rented an apartment on West End Avenue and 93rd Street to pursue purchasing a brownstone. Finally, I bought a brownstone on West 95th Street and lived there for three years. I then purchased a Coop on East 65th Street. I followed that purchase with the purchase of another Coop on East 16th Street three years later. I was the only African American living in these Coops. I then bought another Coop on East 16th Street.

Through my experience with these moves, I wanted to live in Harlem. My next house was in Harlem on 118th Street. I was finally able to feel a connection to the community there. After another three years, I purchased my most challenging and, at the same time, my most desired home on Lenox Avenue. It was a building, a corner brownstone, that seemed to speak to me each time I passed it. Seeking the ownership, I met with the then owner, a

Fearless

White woman who lived in Queens, with many rooming houses in Harlem. Through her and others, I found this to be a pattern. Many people, predominantly White, owned houses in Harlem but had residences outside of the community, mainly in Queens.

I had no idea of the challenges this house would bring to me as I sought to live there. One of the other things I knew nothing about was the perils of small home ownership and "rent control." The key to rent control's political appeal lies as much in its restrictions on eviction as in its capping of rents. Artificially low rents mean little to no tenants unless they can keep their apartments. I had tenants paying rents of $35 per month, or the highest was, I believe, about $90 per month. My tenants were not political, but they learned quickly once I became the owner of the building and they learned that I bought it to live in it with my family. So they stopped paying rent and took me to court for many violations that were on the building when I purchased it. Their legal aid attorney fought for them with a vengeance.

Like many Harlem buildings, my home was divided into rooms, designating it as a "rooming house." Tenants lived in rooms. This was unheard of and totally misunderstood by me, coming from my limited knowledge of housing in Harlem during the 80s.

Joan Oby Dawson

On one of my frequent visits to Baton Rouge, my father became ill and ended up in the hospital. I was happy to be able to sit with him and visit during my stay. Sitting in the hospital by my father's bedside, I reflected on my decision to leave Baton Rouge and move to New York, away from my family. I was not the first of my generation to move out. However, Louisianans did not move to New York. They went to California or Texas. The hospital in Baton Rouge was on Essen Lane. Through the years, as Daddy aged, he had diabetes, he had one leg amputated due to an automobile accident, and he had smoked Lucky Strike cigarettes all of his adult life, causing him to suffer from a chronic cough and congestion. I came to visit him and thoroughly enjoyed our conversations for three days before he slipped into a coma. *"What can I do?"* I thought. I did not want to leave him in a coma, but I was scheduled to leave to keep a court date in New York. I had planned to leave the next day, not knowing that he was going into a coma.

My visit home was in the middle of an ongoing challenge in New York, just for survival. This battle was personal and upfront. While in New York, fighting in the court to keep my home, I received a call that I needed to come home immediately. I did. I spent two extra days going to the hospital to see Daddy. I sat next to his bedside and prayed for him to speak, but he didn't. It was an extremely sad time for me. My scheduled court date in New York

placed me in an immense dilemma. Mother and Daddy did not know of the battle I was in to save my home. I pretended like everything was fine in front of them. I could not imagine this kind of thing happening in Louisiana, and I did not want them to know about it. I guess I was embarrassed and, at the same time, believed that problems grow when given attention. My parents thought of me as a successful woman living my success story. They were proud of me and my accomplishments in New York. After all, they were the ones who did not want me to leave Louisiana in the first place. I did not want to spoil that feeling in them that I had fought to establish for years.

After trying to get me to come home, they finally began to visit and see what they thought was a young woman working, going out in New York City, taking care of her children, and living the life they had hoped for me. So, I hid the elements of my being caught up in the laws of the State that claimed that I could not evict my tenants but had to provide housing for them forever. The court battle was one I could never have imagined. Missing work, crying at night, being served papers on Saturdays and Sundays by the legal aid attorney representing the ten tenants, who ignored the law and seemed to have taken a personal interest in destroying me – it was all so overwhelming for me. I was threatened with contempt of court, and none of the tenants paid rent. Inspectors were in my home on a regular basis, adding violations and requiring a constant

drain on my teacher's salary.

I strategized in every way possible to win over the system. I visited elected officials, and I networked with other small property owners who were in similar battles. I fought as hard as I could to keep the courts from providing an "administrator," someone who takes over your home and can put you out if they wish. I was in a real quandary. I did not want to leave my father, but if I didn't, I might return to New York, and the City of New York may have seized my home.

My father died two days after I arrived back in New York to keep a court date on Friday that ended up being postponed until later. On Saturday, I received the call that my Daddy had passed. I was devastated, but I had to continue to go to court and deal with the great challenge of saving my home. I also understood the plight of my tenants.

I learned that without "rent control," my tenants would have to compete with countless other potential tenants for below-market rentals or pay a higher rent. Some were on welfare or held menial or no jobs. None of this information was available to me, nor did I seek it before my purchase. This was my first purchase of a brownstone with tenants living in it. It became a nightmare that lasted ten years before I could claim victory in reclaiming my home.

I had no idea that the rent control scheme could restrict

evictions in New York in a way that almost no other state implements. However, there is usually an exception for "owner occupancy" evictions, where the landlord seeks to occupy the premises personally. These owner-occupancy provisions were a strange bit of nostalgia. Having eviscerated property rights, the state turned around and tipped its hat to its memory – it may not allow a building owner to do very much with the property, but at least it will let her live in it, or so I thought.

Long before my move, however, New York State decided that even this was going too far. It amended New York City's rent control law to prohibit owner-occupancy evictions of tenants who were elderly or disabled or who had resided in their buildings for more than 20 years. The law took effect immediately upon passage. Having purchased my rent-controlled building expecting to live with my family of four eventually, I found my plans smashed overnight with the change of law. This law applied to all of my tenants except one who moved out without ever paying rent.

This new law went into effect seven months after I bought my dream home. My dream of a single-family home was destroyed by a law that essentially stated that I could not evict rent-controlled tenants. Although this law was enacted after I attempted to go for owner-occupancy, my plans were not retroactive.

Joan Oby Dawson

With the leadership of Competitive Enterprise Institute and Sam Kazman as lead counsel, we filed a lawsuit in the New York State Supreme Court, challenging the law as an uncompensated taking of my property. My case, as explained to me by Mr. Kazman, was a straight constitutional challenge to the 20-year provision of the new law. Although an important precedent, we lost the case. The court ruled that there was an essential difference between our situation and the major cases invalidating housing regulations as taking grounds – specifically, the Supreme Court's.

Needless to say, the state's argument with my family was weird. I bought a house with tenants who, under the law, could have been evicted. Seven months later, the new law turned them into permanent tenants. In other words, I was awarded by the State seven adult people who were previously removable. Still, I, a teacher who sent my children to college so they could care for themselves, was designated a landlord and a caretaker.

None of the tenants had jobs or employable status. They were more or less living on subsidies from the government! The state also attacked me for thinking that the owner-occupied eviction law would stay on the books. It claimed that, given rent control's higher regulated nature and its continuing trend toward tenant-protective measures, it was obligated to assure increased protection for tenants. I

would not imagine that the law would remain fixed, allowing me to own my property paid for with my teacher's salary. In short, there could be no legitimate expectation for owner occupancy under the new rent control, even for the small property owner. *Anything goes if you are a small owner in New York during this time.*

My attorneys surmised that rent control does many things. In many instances, its target is aimed at the wrong people. As it presently stands, Kazman wrote, *"As Swedish economist Assar Lindbeck put it, the most efficient technique known for destroying a city short of bombing. At the social level, it has turned landlords and tenants into permanently warring parties, and it has made the apartment (who gets it? Who keeps it?) The defining feature of thousands of lives and relationships."* At the individual level, my level, as a small property owner, it had had an extraordinary impact on my life and that of my family.

New York City instituted rent control 70 years ago as a temporary solution to a temporary housing shortage. What a temporary fix! As for me, the New York Appellate Division ruled against me. The court held that given rent control's expanding nature, my family should have known better than to rely on existing law when I purchased my home. This reasoning conveniently ignored the fact that the very purpose of the Fifth Amendment, assuring the right of

property ownership without the threat of it being taken for public use without just compensation, was to restrain such an expansion. As stated by Kazman, *"Justice Holmes noted more than three quarters of a century ago the compensation requirement is intended to check the very natural tendency of human nature, to extend the regulation more and more until at last private property disappears."*

New York's highest court ruled against us, and the US Supreme Court refused to review it. We finally paid our tenants money to vacate. The last tenant was paid after she changed her name. It was unclear whether this was legally permitted since she was on welfare and could not collect the full $10,000 amount negotiated by Legal Aid. She got a windfall, having never paid rent since she learned that we wanted the house for the family.

Despite these challenges, there was always help. Sam Kazman of the Competitive Enterprise Institute and his law firm took our case pro bono. I am incredibly grateful for the work they did and the knowledge gained. My family won, even though the verdict seemed not in our favor. There was other help. A lot of it!

"Behold I send you forth as sheep in the mist of wolves; be ye therefore wise as serpents, and harmless as doves."

- Matthew 10:16

Fearless

Joan Oby Dawson

Chapter XIII
Purpose

    To attempt to change an entire system of school failure is no small feat and cannot be done by any one individual. The problem is systemic and it must be attacked systemically. My children, having a sound beginning in a segregated system in Baton Rouge, were doing well, however, the children in the New York school system were failing academically, and that bothered me. Sitting in meetings and hearing people in charge comfortably brag about 65%, 70%, and even 80% success rates made me wonder about the other 20% or 30%. What about those children? What was their plight in life? It always amazed me when I visited schools in Scarsdale and other upscale areas like Cherry Hill or Phillipsburg, New Jersey, and Upstate New York. Their rich resources mystified me, especially when compared to the lack of resources for children in Harlem schools or the poor school districts in New Jersey. These differences were the highlight of the continuation of "separate but supposedly equal." There was nothing equal about the circumstances that surrounded the children of poverty or poor neighborhoods. Could these differences in resources have anything to do with the quality of the educational process and the outcomes of students?

Fearless

The education of children and youth evolved as my core purpose and my cornerstone. It was as if their education became a driving force behind my efforts. Perhaps it was because much of my career and my life revolved around the education of children and youth. Whether in Baton Rouge, a small town, or in New York, a metropolitan city, the largest school district in the country, my main focus remained the same: to create a better learning experience for children, especially those who faced challenges while communicating. Observing a positive change in a child who experienced communication challenges would always bring me joy. As I continued to work in that field, I learned much more than I taught. I learned that parents loved their children regardless of circumstances. Since the failures in schools across the country seemed to impact the African American population negatively, I turned to the policies that guided the instruction of that population.

One such policy was the development of the multicultural education policy, a pivotal turning point in the history of our country. I found many flaws. Something that was aimed at making the system better for all children was the very thing that was filled with flaws. Before my work at NYU, I was basing my speculations on observation and personal experiences. My job at NYU informed me of some of the invisible underpinnings faced by the students and parents, which I dealt with on a daily basis by looking at

the data scientifically. I conducted extensive research on the City and its plans for addressing the needs of African American children. My research extended to the part their history played in their intellectual development within the New York City School System.

Educators in New York City began focusing on multicultural education in the 1960s and 70s as ethnic studies became popular in colleges and universities. Having just arrived in NYC, I realized that multicultural education issues were first perceived as a way to respond to the culture of African American students. However, as the boundaries of multicultural education extended, by the mid to late 70s, issues ranged from strict curriculum reform to issues of race, class, and gender inequities.

In 1989, the New York City Board of Education adopted a policy on multicultural education. That policy has gone through several revisions since. The 1989 policy reflected the Board's position, emphasizing that if schools were to accept cultural diversity as a valuable resource, then each stakeholder would have a certain responsibility. That responsibility would include school personnel, parents, and students to pay attention and be able to recognize subtle and blatant biased attitudes and actions that lead to discrimination on the basis of race, color, religion, national origin, gender, age, sexual orientation, and handicapping conditions.

I began to understand the reason for my uncertain and disturbing feelings when I saw angry children continuing to fail in a system designed for failure in such a perplexing format that it was not easy for anyone to understand or uncover.

There was confusion even among those who agreed that there was a need for a multicultural education system where resources were equitable and teaching staff had compassion for the students they were teaching. The development of this policy faced a massive amount of disagreement.

This did not keep people silent. Parents and interest groups continued to speak out about their concerns not being addressed on this issue. There were questions from parents about what was being taught to their children in the curriculum. As a result of growing discontent in communities across the City, issues of curriculum fueled the 1993 races for school boards across the City. Candidates backed by coalitions of religious and other groups were nurtured not only by Cardinal O'Connor of the Archdiocese of New York but also by a broad and popular coalition. Queens Borough President Clare Schulman's office was flooded with protest calls from Protestants, Catholics, and Jewish groups. City-wide protests came from Muslims, Russian immigrants, Black Baptists, and Pentecostal and Catholic Hispanics.

Much of the debate raging all over the City was over the extent to which students should be exposed to homosexual lifestyles when schools teach tolerance. However, it also assumed larger and more subtle dimensions. For example, in District 15, which included brownstone neighborhoods like Park Slope and working-class districts like Sunset Park, the debate reflected divisions between advocates of back-to-basics schooling. Those who favored innovative teaching styles often leaned toward prioritizing what is perceived as working-class and middle-class values. They may also have differing perspectives on the role of schools as dispensers of sex education and condoms, with this division sometimes aligning along the lines of often liberal Whites and frequently conservative Hispanic people.

The protests were becoming more frequent with each passing day. Parents in the Sunset Park section of Brooklyn marched up Fifth Avenue to protest the handling of the issue by District 15, causing the district to suspend the part of the curriculum that dealt with homosexuality. On the other hand, the gay groups, which represented an increasingly influential voting block in the city, enlisted politicians to strengthen their decision influence. Elected officials who had a history of support for gay causes, from Mayor Dinkins to Borough President Ruth Messenger, voiced their support for the curriculum guide. Interest groups throughout the City surfaced to support or oppose

the curriculum guide, stirring this matter further.

Unfortunately, as with any new approach to education, some found that too many practitioners were perhaps eager to become involved without taking the time to understand the philosophy or rationale behind the approach itself. That resulted in a variety of projects and programs that had little to do with the process of implementing multicultural education. It should have been developed based on the experience and history of this nation. Such processes are consistent with how we view the relationship between school and society and the history of impacted students, and so they should be.

The policy met with the waters of uncertainty as players came in and went out of the system. With each new arrival or departure, rules were changed. This kept changing the message that was being sent to the parents and the students who held hopes in the light of this policy. As a result, there was no lasting policy.

Throughout the decade (1985-1995), the rise in the number of African American, Hispanic, and poor and failing students in the New York City school system was steady. In 1989, at the time of the adoption of the policy of multicultural education, when New York State singled out its 43 most troubled schools, 31 were in New York City.

The system was filled with incompetence, lack of

consistency, and frequent changes in leadership, thereby causing changes in behavior with each shift in staff and a multitude of other flaws that interfered with its purpose. There were still some good elements in the system. though: dedicated parents and teachers were there and still are to try and make good happen. For years, there seemed to be no lasting purpose. Or perhaps it was extremely unclear and ever-changing.

We now live in a culture where the entire system continues to shift goals, ideals, and ideas, leading to instability and uncertainty. How can the system stand? It cannot! But it will! There are debates going on among our elected leaders regarding something called Critical Race Theory. No one seems to have a consistent idea of the theory. I would be willing to bet that if you asked ten people to define Critical Race Theory, you would get ten radically different definitions.

According to the NAACP Legal Defense Fund, Critical Race Theory originated in the 1970s and is defined as an academic and legal framework that denotes the systemic racism that is engrained in our American society. Some of us know it as understanding the origin of systemic racism. It is embedded in the laws, policies, and institutions that uphold and reproduce racial inequalities.

Policies that attempt to conceal the truth of the

contributions of the African American cultures to the building of this great country, including New York City, are a way of denying power where power is due. Our children and youth represent that power.

While having dinner with my son and his friends, the wall of the restaurant was flanked with posters of jockeys and horses. One of the guests said, "Where are the African American jockeys?" Another answered, "They are probably not to be seen except for leading the horses out to the White jockeys who will race them." Having heard this and knowing it to be an example of unknown history, I immediately went to my phone and looked up the topic of African American jockeys.

One of the advantages of technology is that knowledge is at one's fingertips. I proudly announced, "Back in 1898, a jockey named Willie Simms not only won all of the Triple Crown Races, claiming victory at the Kentucky Derby, which he won twice, but he also won the Belmont Stakes and the Preakness Stakes. He was also the first jockey to win a race in England on an American horse." We discovered that there were many other African American jockeys during that time. This history was not known to us as adults.

There were inequities in the health care system where the mortality rate of certain groups was higher than that of

the other groups, which has its roots in this system. Inadequate textbooks, libraries, technology, programs, the arts, exercise in our schools, and even space are related. These issues pertain to both policy-making and legal matters, hence leading to denial in legal terms. It is the oblivion of the history of their roots that makes people feel defeated, leading them to perish. Having knowledge of our history is crucial in ensuring that it is never erased. That should just not happen.

A power shift is taking place. Nonetheless, the good news is that the "genie cannot be put back into the bottle." The egg is broken and cannot be put together again. We are out of slavery, never to return. Many of us were never in slavery but had to face similar circumstances anyway. There were many people of African descent in the deep southern states who were free and never enslaved. Louisiana is one of those states. At the nexus of slavery and freedom were free people of color, the tens of thousands of people of African descent who overcame incredible odds and lived free in the most unlikely of places – the slave societies of the South, the Caribbean, and Latin America – in the 18th and early 19th centuries.

If most Americans today were aware that some African men and women, like Fredrick Douglass and Harriet Tubman, were able to escape from southern plantations and live in freedom in the North, only a few would realize that

free African Americans also lived in and occasionally prospered in places where slavery was so deeply rooted that it took a war to abolish it. One such place was Louisiana.

While at NYU, I delved into the policy of multicultural education and its stages of development to find out why our history was not being systematically taught. The findings were mindboggling. For example, did you know the truth about the policy being so convoluted that every time a new change occurred, the policy would receive a hit, change in the process, and never remain the same or develop into a lasting version? I am sure that it is still happening as we attempt to educate our youth and others about our history.

The entire history and culture of African Americans in this country had been diluted by other stories being mixed in. For example, in 1991, when the Children of the Rainbow was released into the school system under the direction of Chancellor Fernandez, some questionable content was added to the curriculum without the knowledge of those who contributed to the final draft. Books like "Heather Has Two Mommies" and "Daddy's Roommate" were included without explanation. The committee was caught off guard, according to one of the committee members. They understood that the fight had to be waged for gays and lesbians, but this was not the original intent of the policy. The truth needed to be told about the History of the African Americans in this country. To mix the two

pieces up because of the gay and lesbian controversy caused a change in the agenda, and they never developed a meaningful policy on multicultural education. Now, that's where we are battling Critical Race Theory.

Consequently, groups became broiled down into Children of the Rainbow. It took center stage. The process of telling the truth about the history of African people and Native people in this country never happened. People like Shelia Evans Tranman and others were leaders in this fight for the truth.

"Remember the former things of old, for I am God, and there is none like me. Teaching the end from the beginning, and from ancient times the things that are not yet done,"

- Isaiah 46:9

Chapter XIV
Friendship

My parents agreed to keep my children while I studied at NYU. "I will only stay there for a year," I told my mother. I think they knew that I needed the time. However, while in New York, I explored work, housing, and other issues that were necessary when I chose to move there permanently. The Board of Education was ready to hire me then, but since I was only there for a year at this time, I was inclined towards declining the offer. However, there was a change of plans later on. Besides, I had a lot on my hands, one being the matter of housing. I was battling for something I knew nothing of. Housing in New York City was a sort of knowledge that I was oblivious to.

After all, I was living in Judson Hall, a dormitory at NYU, so how could I have known more? However, I did take a small apartment for a short period, which I sublet when my mother brought my children up to visit me during that year of study.

I realized, without ever stating it, that I was destined to live in New York. In fact, I actually thought it would be good for me and even better for my children. There were so many things for children to do. The museums, the Central Park Zoo, the Bronx Zoo, Central Park itself, and the

Planetarium. Apart from those fascinating places, there were many programs designed for children, which all seemed perfect for my two kids. I had already visited for a year, applied for a job with the New York City Board of Education, and began exploring appropriate housing. I went back to Baton Rouge to give myself time to reflect on the wisdom of the move to New York. That year in New York was good for me. My daughter remarked that when I came to visit them during the year they were with my mother, I was wearing a mini dashiki, and all of my hair was cut off. I had gone natural and sported a short afro. The transition had already begun.

New York was different from Louisiana. In fact, it was far different.

I accepted the position with the New York City Board of Education as a speech pathologist. I lived in the Bronx with former Mayfair neighbors (my children's play cousins) who were in the restaurant business until I could get an apartment in their building. I knew no one else in New York. They took my children and me in for about a month until an apartment became available in the same building. I never liked the Bronx. It was not like Manhattan, which was my previous introduction to New York, but it was a roof over our heads.

Working as a speech pathologist was routine. I went to

Fearless

work and showed up at one school three days a week and another two days a week. My schedule included a caseload of 10-15 elementary school children per day who were identified as in need of language services. They were seen in groups of three or individually, depending upon what was specified in an IEP that was determined by someone else. The principal was responsible for providing the speech pathologist and any other service provider with a workplace in the school to see the children. One of my school principals provided me with a small room about the size of a closet with no windows. The other assigned me a room behind the gym. I believe it was an equipment room.

These assignments continued until the Superintendent asked me if I would like to change programs and work as a paraprofessional trainer. That was a position created to train parents who worked in schools to upgrade the skills that they needed to appropriate excellent or at least better performances in the classrooms. This led to the development of a career ladder program where many of them became teachers, and a few became principals. Later, I worked in several other roles, including Principal of an Alternative School, Curriculum Developer, Reading Specialist, and other related roles as the superintendent determined.

While working on my first assignment as a speech pathologist, I met Jackie, who became a lasting friend. I

was in a room that was so small yet boisterous, located behind the gym. It had to be an equipment room based on its size. Students were running up and down, throwing and bouncing a basketball, which made it difficult for me to concentrate and made me realize that there was no way that I could successfully work with the children assigned to me. I looked up to see a young woman coming my way. She was attractive and carrying a stack of papers. She walked into the room where I was seated behind the one desk in the room. "Hello," we both said at the same time.

"I'm Jackie," she said, introducing herself.

"I'm Joan," I replied.

We both looked at each other to try to figure out what was going on. Jackie then explained to me that she was the bilingual teacher for the school. Her assignment was to assist the large Hispanic population of students in assimilating and adapting to the school environment. This included helping them learn English so that they could adapt to the classroom work.

It appeared that Jackie was assigned to the same room as me during one of the three days I was to be there. The school was dilapidated and was not attractive in the least. It was nothing like the new schools in Baton Rouge where I worked. The schools were old, with narrow hallways, old equipment, and books that were worn out and tattered.

Fearless

Jackie and I shared many common interests; our families were large and engaging, and we had children. Although we were not similar in age, we had similar upbringings within a large family. My children were instant babysitters for her little girl, Jamie.

Since Jackie was a bilingual teacher, her assignment was to help the Hispanic children learn English fluently. She was brought up in New York, yet her ties remained intact with her Puerto Rican family heritage, which led her to be fluent in Spanish and not just English.

Since we were in charge of our own schedules, we decided that we would work two days and share on the third day. The principal stated that there was no other room available. The room was really not appropriate for the work either of us did. We competed with the sounds of basketballs bouncing, children yelling, and coaches giving directions throughout the time, so we needed a quiet room to help the children. Some of the time, the room was quiet when a gym class was not in session.

Jackie ended up asking me to go out with her to celebrate the divorce of her first husband. We ended up at her mother, Ina's house, where I fell in love with Puerto Rican food.

Over the years, Jackie and I became good friends. Our children got to know each other, and our families became

entangled. Jackie visited Baton Rouge, and I visited Ponce, the town she was from in Puerto Rico. Ina, Jackie's mother, became an extension of my own family. I don't quite remember when Jackie met her second husband, but she did marry and had a son named Ralph.

I have no idea how Jackie met her third husband. It seemed to me that she had no trouble meeting and marrying. I, on the other hand, was extremely cautious about taking that step of marriage or even getting seriously involved.

Jackie's third husband was a doctor from Baltimore. To be specific, he was a gynecologist who also had another gynecologist friend. That friend and I dated for some time until he conveniently died of a sudden heart attack. Since I was not really the marrying kind, I enjoyed going out with Jackie and her new husband. We spent a lot of time together, and Jackie insisted that I be included in most of the activities that she and Jose planned.

Jackie's wedding plans moved into full swing very quickly. Although she had only known Jose for the past year, she was suddenly being pressured by him to get married soon. Although separated, he was not yet divorced from his wife of a previous marriage. The divorce was pending. He wanted Jackie to begin plans for marriage during his legal separation. Jackie's husband was living

Fearless

alone after 15 years of living with his previous wife, raising three boys and a girl, the oldest 14 and the youngest six. "Living alone, except for visits from my children, is uncomfortable and lonely," he expressed.

The men made the topic of gynecology the topic of many of their jokes. These jokes almost always came up when we were in pubs or bars or even over dinner. Jackie and I were offended by the nature of these jokes about women's anatomy and the advantages or sometimes disadvantages of the gynecological profession. However, neither she nor I ever spoke on the offense.

Jackie chose to leave her position as a teacher and board member in the Bronx and become a full-time housewife. She and her husband found themselves discussing this matter, which led the couple to reach a compromise. In light of that discussion, Jackie left both positions and took a teaching position in Cherry Hill, New Jersey, where they settled, away from New York and away from his home in Baltimore.

A ceremony was planned for the wedding in Puerto Rico. I was her maid of honor while I was also scheduled to participate in a conference in Apia, Western Samoa, a week after the wedding. *"How am I going to do this?"* I thought. *"I'll make it work,"* I told myself.

For me, the beautiful wedding was another opportunity

to travel. I had been to Puerto Rico before with Jackie, but this was special. On August 15th, in Ponce, Puerto Rico, Jackie became Ms. Jackie with a string of names following, representing her two first husbands and all of the names that were attached to the culture associated with her Hispanic origin.

Surprisingly, during the preparations and while running here and there to make sure everything was perfect and while rummaging Canal Street, Manhattan, to get her wedding dress as well as for her maid of honor – me, we both were struck by a realization. Jackie and I were committed to several projects. Being too committed to projects of our own, distinct as they were, we both realized that we were growing apart.

Without discussion, we realized that our interests were changing. Marriage and living in Cherry Hill were only two of those factors. I still enjoyed traveling, and Jackie had less time. I was looking forward to the trip to the South Pacific, and Jackie was looking forward to making new friends and finding a new home away from New York. I was also missing the mark in my personal development with God. I thought, *"I cannot discuss this because I don't yet understand what's missing."*

Despite these changes, our commitment to each other did not change. The wedding was spectacular, and the

reception took place in the hills of Ponce Puerto in a restaurant that seemed to be a part of heaven. We began seeing each other less frequently since I traveled with groups. Sometimes, I would be alone, and other times, I would be on a date. I went to several countries in Africa a few times. In fact, I visited several Islands too, like Bermuda, Aruba, and others, the names of which I cannot recall. Then, there were my visits to Mexico, Spain, Dubai, Israel, Italy, Malta, London, Paris, and several other places throughout the world. And, of course, while working at New York University, in my role as Director of the Equity Assistance Center, I worked in St. Thomas, St. Croix, St. John, and Puerto Rico on a regular basis.

"I lift up my eyes to the hills, from whence cometh my help. My help cometh from the Lord which made heaven and earth."

- Psalm 121

Joan Oby Dawson

Chapter XV
Boldness

After leaving Puerto Rico, I flew off the following day to Los Angeles to spend a night with Yvonne and then off to Apia, Western Samoa. This trip has a special kind of significance in my life. I would love to share some of the details of that trip with you. So here's how everything went.

I arrived in Pago Pago, American Samoa, on Tuesday morning around six. The flight to American Samoa was direct from Honolulu. After a four-hour layover in Honolulu, I realized that I would have to accept the description of the Island given by the pilot as the plane descended just before landing.

The trip was a relatively quiet one. As the women in the airport began to talk, I realized that many of the passengers on the flight from California were also in route to the Women's Conference in Apia. The flight also picked up women in Hawaii since there was also a Japanese delegation at the airport. Some Hawaiians were waiting to board the plane. New Yorkers were easily identifiable. They were more assertive, somewhat louder, and more aggressive. Upon spotting a New Yorker based on these characteristics, I approached her and introduced myself as a

Fearless

New Yorker, too.

Thanks to her aggressiveness, she and I were whisked through the immigration line very quickly. She was one of those few women who were neither traveling with a group nor with a delegation. I was the only African American woman traveling to the conference. Nonetheless, there were a few Hawaiian women who were brown or olive in complexion.

There were some advantages of being the only African American on the trip. I was hand-picked to go first on all of the lines. A handsome young agent came out of nowhere, quickly took my bag, and whisked me around other lines, ushering me in front of long lines of women waiting to get through. He then processed my luggage while a few of the women complained, even taking a long time to move into position to board the plane to Pago Pago.

Whatever advantages arose, I appreciated them and did not comment since I had had little sleep since the wedding, and the trip from Puerto Rico to Hawaii was almost 24 hours.

We arrived in Apia, Western Samoa, one hour after leaving Pago Pago. We were greeted by an entourage of beautiful island women dancing and singing and placing a beautiful flower in each guest's hair. The flower was placed on the left side if the woman was single and on the right

side if married. Of course, my flower was placed on the left.

Jane's Tour Service picked us up. The people of Samoa were, for the most part, beautiful people. Jane was no exception. The New York delegation of five women was driven to the Aggie Gray's hotel, situated pleasantly across the street from the sea. Aggie Gray, in her 80s, still lived in the hotel.

This hotel reminded me of the large mansions in Louisiana. The several steps up to the massive front doors were flanked with banisters on each side, leaving room for the many early dawn-filled dewy mornings. I sat there watching the small boats of the Samoan men going out to fish at sea. Undoubtedly, it was all picturesque and mystical.

Upon entering the double front doors, the huge foyer opened to a large informal room with over-stuffed, comfortable seating and a display of bulletins highlighting activities and appointments for the week. On the other side of this room was a casual dining room, including additional seating for just lounging or relaxation. Beyond the foyer, the dining room, and the informal seating, a series of steps led down to an outdoor bar with tables and chairs. The entire outdoor lounge area was encompassed by a courtyard of fruit-bearing trees such as bananas, oranges, papaya, and

Fearless

beautiful flowers, forming a border of delicacies for viewing or partaking. The path along the border led to the guest's accommodations.

I showered, got dressed, and decided to take a walk. "How beautiful," I thought as I moved along with the Pacific Ocean on one side and the town of Apia on the other. "What a beautiful part of the world – a remarkable creation of God," I mused.

For the remainder of my stay, my ritual became one of walking along the Pacific Ocean at 6 am every morning while engaging in short conversations with the Samoans. I came across people going to work who looked like my aunts and uncles. These people had beautiful skins but were curious about African Americans. They asked me about two things: One was about Harlem and crime, and the other was about Martin Luther King.

During these walks and conversations with the Samoan people, I learned that the Samoan family had a social, economic, and cultural system that was linguistically different but similar to my Southern culture. There was a head of the family called the Matai, and the family included the extended family, consisting of grandparents, cousins, aunts, uncles, and in-laws, and the family went on and on. The Matai was the chief or head who made all of the decisions for the family members. The position was

bestowed upon a highly respected and intelligent man or woman. The Matai was determined by all of the members of the family. There was a difference between the Matai I have in my family and the Matai of Samoan families. The difference was that the Matai owned all the land and determined the family rules. In my family, individuals own land. It also seemed that there was a rule according to which the Matai settled disputes, from marriage disagreements, children's problems, and economic and social disputes among brothers and sisters.

Women in Samoa held a significant number of political positions. The women's conference had begun even before the New York delegation arrived. Exhibits of Island crafts were appealing and expensive. The conference meetings were like any of the many conferences I had attended, so I spent time browsing, attending some meetings, listening to speakers, and preparing for my own brief talk that was scheduled a couple of days after my arrival.

Jane of Jane's Tours was around all the time. "Let's have lunch together," Jane approached me at the craft table. "Sounds good," I responded. During that first week, I roamed around the Island, socialized with the women who attended the conference, talked with the Samoan women and men, and shared personal life stories. The festive celebrations were held all over the Island. The most

prominent ones were held right at Aggie Gray's. One of the most fascinating things to watch was the Samoan dance. It was not at all like dance in the United States. The movement was beautiful and exotic. Minimal body movement, mostly the hands and shoulders, seemed to move with majesty and extremely suggestive graceful communication. The famed Aggie Gray was always present to bring to life the romantic legend of her heritage. It seemed that she had fallen in love with a young Samoan man when she was a young woman, only to have him die at an early age. She had accepted and embodied the Samoan culture and remained in the hotel that was previously their home.

The day of my short remarks was uneventful. I was limited to twenty minutes and unable to cover much of what I had prepared. However, after having many conversations, explorations, and socialization with the people of the Island, I knew exactly what they wanted from me, and I was ready to deliver. I spoke of the African American family in general, letting them know there was no "cookie cutter version" to our existence in the United States. I tried to dispel many of the myths I had heard in discussions during the week. The image of drugs, poverty, disorganization, crime, and other negatives was replaced with education, strength, economic development, determination, and faith. After the talk, I was mobbed by women wanting me to visit or Samoan men wanting to

show me around Samoa.

The following day, after my usual walk, I sat outside the entrance doors to the hotel, meditating and thinking about the departure from such a beautiful experience. It was quite early – perhaps, seven in the morning. A new guest was arriving at the hotel. There seemed to be a surge of excitement among the hotel staff pertaining to the arrival of this new guest. A black limo came and was parked right in front of the hotel gates. Several White men stepped out of it and then scurried into the hotel. The new guest was Mr. Daly.

Mr. Daly slowly removed himself from the back of the limo with the assistance of the driver. Riley, a white-haired, stately man, accompanied Mr. Daly but quickly moved ahead, directing staff to remove the unending suitcases and trunks from the car. Paloma, the driver, was a Samoan. I found out later that he worked for the Samoan government. However, while Mr. Daly was present, his job was to specifically drive Mr. Daly, protect him, wait on him, and do his bidding during his visit.

Mr. Daly wore a white suit, white hat, and white shoes. His thin white hair was cropped just below the rim of the hat while the man wore dark shades. He passed me on the stoop, nodded, and continued into the hotel.

Another member of the entourage was another White

man, Brian. Brian appeared to be the one who took care of all business. He spoke at the desk; he seemed attached to a black briefcase that he did not trust to anyone – even the staff who attempted to add it to the other luggage. They all disappeared behind closed doors very quickly.

On my way back to the hotel, I spotted Aggie Gray having coffee and breakfast in the outer courtyard. I decided to go over and introduce myself to her. She looked up at me and smiled, gesturing me to sit and join her. I did. Aggie Gray was pleasant and curious. While we were talking, Mr. Daly, the man in the white suit, approached and asked if he could join. Mr. Daly was introduced as the President of World Airways. He had been a benefactor of the Island of Samoa for many years. He had earned quite the reputation as a man who built hospitals, hired flight attendants, and contributed in other ways to improving the welfare of the Samoans. He was honored and respected by the people of Samoa and was there to go on a trip to one of the other Islands.

After some unplanned conversation ensued, Mr. Daly extended an invitation to me to accompany his party on the trip. I declined, being a bit hesitant. I was scheduled to leave later that day since the women's conference was over.

"He will not let your foot be moved, he who keeps you will not slumber. He will not let you stumble."

Joan Oby Dawson

– Psalm 121: 3

Chapter XVI
Light and Easy

That same day, I met Jane for lunch. It was not surprising at all to see Jane ordering the Aggie Gray special, an Island drink named after Aggie Gray. As we sipped on the rum-based fruity drink, we talked about New York and my return.

"Did you meet Mr. Daly?" Jane inquired.

"Yes, I did," I answered.

"I'm sorry you have to leave so early," said Jane. "You should stay longer," she continued. "You haven't had time to enjoy the Island. Some of the young men asked about you. They would like to take you to the local spots on the Island, the ones tourists don't know about."

"Besides, Mr. Daly has a three-day trip planned for tomorrow." Jane continued. "He has done so much for the Island and the people here."

"Yes, I know," I replied. "He invited me to come along."

"What?!" Jane almost shouted. "Then why are you

going home?" She asked in amazement.

"Jane, I don't want to spend any more money," I explained.

"Joan, Mr. Daly is worth about 30 million dollars," Jane stated between her teeth. "He's a gentleman and a very good person. Please reconsider."

Jane suddenly became a woman with a mission after I agreed that the trip might be nice. As we were sipping on our second drink, Brian, the briefcase man, walked through the lobby. Jane approached him and told him that I had reconsidered Mr. Daly's offer and would like to go on the trip. She told him that I had already checked out of my room, so that would have to be taken care of. Brian handled all arrangements for hotel accommodations and whatever else was needed for me to go on the trip.

Jane left but called the next morning to make sure things were taken care of. I met with Brian in the courtyard, where he showed me albums of Mr. Daly's involvement in the Pacific Islands. All the while, he was on the phone, making arrangements for speaking engagements and appearances at certain events on the other Islands and in Apia. A new wing of the children's hospital was scheduled to open later during the week. And, of course, Mr. Daly was the speaker. Other photos featured Mr. Daly's flight into Vietnam during the war. There were photographs of

Fearless

people attempting to get on the plane as the plane took off to help people escape the danger of the war. Other photos showed lines of children waiting until the plane returned. I learned that Mr. Daly was criticized for kidnapping, meddling, and unnecessary involvement in the terrible Vietnam War.

Brian asked me to go shopping with him for the trip. "We all need lava lava's. This is the wrap or clothing item to wear on the trip." I enjoyed helping Brian with the shopping for items that would be needed on the trip. We bought four lava lava's, some cleaning supplies, some food, and some wine. Brian had hired two young Samoan girls to do the cooking and cleaning. Adella and Lupi were beautiful young Samoan women, probably in their early twenties or younger. Lupi's mother had approached me in the hotel lobby and asked me to "Look after my daughter." I responded, "Of course I will." Apparently, all of the Islanders knew that I was going on the trip with Mr. Daly.

As we returned, Brian said that he had to check out the boat. Mr. Daly had also hired a young couple from California with a trimaran to accompany us so that we could go from the ship to the sailboat at will. After all this, I went to my room to relax. I needed to rest a bit since we were boarding that night at around dusk.

Paloma, the driver, drove Brian and me to the dock to

examine the boat. Brian looked shocked. The boat Mr. Daly wanted was unavailable, but he was not easily dissuaded when he wanted to do something. Since the boat he wanted was not available, he instructed the company to complete the repair of one that had not been in use for a while. He would not delay his planned trip. However, he had apparently planned it without the company knowing that.

The cook Mr. Daly hired quit after seeing the condition of the kitchen. The very large boat, apparently once elegant, was in shambles. It was dirty, and the toilets were filled with dirt and, in some instances, clogged. The boat appeared to not have been in use for years. Adella and Lupi needed forewarning of what was in front of them regarding cleaning. They also needed to start early.

On the second shopping trip, Brian and I bought ammonia, cleaning supplies, more toilet paper, and a host of other things. I assured Lupi and Adela that they would enjoy the trip even though the work was not easy. I persuaded Brian to pay them more money for the additional work.

We finally boarded and left at around 6:00 in the evening. Adella took the job of food and serving, and Lupi cleaned, served, and entertained the guests. Lupi, the more outgoing of the two girls, was actually good at entertaining. She told jokes, kidded with the men, including Mr. Daly,

Fearless

and was in and out of the Pacific, swimming with Riley, Larry, and Cynthia, who were the couple on the sailboat. Lupi was quick with her wit and humor yet set a code of respect.

Mr. Daly made his remark to the entire guest staff and crew before departing with glass in hand, and he stated, "The women are in my care. They are to be totally respected, and anyone who does not respect them in any way will be thrown overboard." He then, with his own companion, Mey Ling, went back below to one of the cabins.

Brian and Riley made great companions for me. Riley, who was 55, lived in California, was also a great swimmer. He was married and spoke of his wife often. Riley was strikingly handsome. He was tall and seemed more than six feet. His hair was stark white, full and shaped his face beautifully. He wore a perpetual smile that exhibited humor and mischief. He was easy to talk with and free with information about Mr. Daly. Brian, on the other hand was more serious, worked full time for Mr. Daly, always traveled with him, and worried about his health. Brian was also married, but he never mentioned his wife.

The hired musician, Bunny, played the guitar and sang various songs. I decided to sing one of my favorites as Bunny played. I sang Amazing Grace. We all found various

places to sleep for the night and planned an early start the next morning.

I chose a place on the deck to sleep. We had adequate blankets, sheets, and pillars that had to be changed during the night, because they became damp with the night and early morning mist. Brian and I went up to the deck early to claim two of the available benches. We claimed two that formed an L shape. Our feet met as we lay covered, gazing at the constellation of stars above. It was one of the most beautiful constellations I had ever witnessed. We talked about the stars and found the Milky Way but could not find the Big Dipper and the Little Dipper. We finally concluded that the sky above, when so close to the equator, is totally different from the sky one sees in the United States. All the while, the noise of entertainment continued down in the cabin area. Mr. Daly, Riley, Lupi and the others were being entertained by each other and Bunny.

Upon hearing someone approaching, I recognized Adella, who seemed tired and a bit nervous. Sensing her sleepiness, I asked, "Would you like to lie down and rest?" I asked. Brian immediately gave up his bench, and Adella stretched out on the bench, her feet meeting mine. I covered her up with sheets and blankets, and she was soon fast asleep.

Riley soon joined us on the deck, located an empty

Fearless

bench, and we all slept in the damp mist of the sea.

Around five in the morning, Mr. Daly came up to learn how I was making it as a single woman in New York. I assured him that I was fine. I sometimes regret that I did not share more about myself with him. He seemed generously interested in my welfare.

"What are you going to do with that bucket of ice?" I asked Mr. Daly. "Watch," he replied. He went over to where Riley was, who was sleeping on the opposite bench, and dumped the cubes of ice down Riley's shorts. He woke up everybody and called for the party to continue.

Riley and I went over to the sailboat with Larry and Cynthia. We were finally on our way to Savaii Island. The sun was hot, and the only shade was from the sails. I followed the sails, trying to avoid the direct heat. The water was beautiful. One could see the rocks, the fish, and the corals, which were all visible, as Larry and Cynthia described, from twelve to fourteen fathoms. The land was out of sight, and we alternated between the sailboat and the cruise ship.

Larry and Cynthia sailed from island to island, taking tourists out to sea. Their home was their boat. They shopped for basic necessities wherever they docked.

Cynthia made lunch, which included banana and

homemade peanut butter sandwiches, a fresh salad, and fresh island vegetables.

It was beginning to get late. The wind was still, and the sailboat was adrift for the next seven or eight hours. The cruise ship was nowhere to be seen., neither was land. Larry spotted the ship returning to meet the sailboat. After a rough hitching of the sailboat to the cruise ship, we were led to a village that was one-third of Savaii Island and our destination. We were advised to spend the night in the village because the sea was too rough to continue. A dinghy was sent to fetch us from the ship and take us to the village. I did venture to take a swim in the Pacific Ocean before going to the village, asking Riley to stay close to me in the water. I was determined to swim in the South Pacific before going back to New York. Riley stayed close, but I found swimming in the ocean easier than swimming in the pool. Riley agreed as he remained close.

We spent the night with a family in the village. That night, I slept on an open porch. The house belonged to a couple, Jack and Rosa. Jack worked for the Samoan Government. He was the supervisor of the workers on the coconut, cocoa bean, and coffee plantations. Rosa spoke no English but was extremely friendly and gracious.

We were fed a delicious meal of delicacies, including the traditional pig in the middle of the table, surrounded by

flowers and fruit. Seaweed, taro leaves, coconut fruit bread, raw fish, chicken, guava root, and potato and fish salads were also served.

Mr. Daly was up early the following day again. He woke everybody up, this time more seriously. He had been alerted that the water was too rough to continue, the boat might not hold up, and that we should head back to Apia. Our trip to Savaii was canceled.

The sea was rough on the return trip. Mr. Daly, Mey Ling, Lupi, and Bunny went on the sailboat. Riley, Brian Adella, and I were on the newly designated *African Queen*. The boat was going at a greater speed to get back before the water became even rougher. After about an hour on the water, Brian looked for food. "Where's the food?" he asked.

Adella immediately got up and reported after searching, "There is none."

Riley moved toward the kitchen. "You mean they took all of the food?" he stated in disbelief.

Adella found half a loaf of bread, some mustard, and one can of tuna. We all laughed at the idea of the entire crew and the four of us being fed from one can of tuna and a half loaf of bread.

The sailboat was far behind the ship. Mike, the captain of the crew, decided to hitch the sailboat to the ship so that we could have a better time. The sea was getting rougher, and the waves were causing the boat to rock from side to side. It was even difficult to walk across the floor without falling. Riley decided that the best thing he could do was go to sleep. That he did – in the middle of the floor. Brian and I went to the deck to watch for the sailboat. After some waving and waiting, the sailboat was connected with a rope. The captain resumed considerable speed to return to Apia before dark.

As Brian and I watched the sailboat move through the waters, we noticed Larry and Mr. Daly waving. "Hey, look, they're waving to us," Brian commented.

"Yes," I replied. "They must be enjoying themselves."

We both waved back as the tiny sailboat was splitting the waters behind the big boat.

"Wait," Brian became serious. "I think he's trying to tell us something." He continued, "I'll get Mike."

Mike stopped the boat and found an extremely upset Ed Daly. The choppy waters were even worse for the sailboat as the boat's waves added to the turbulence surrounding it. Not only were they soaked, but they were also being thrown to and fro from the speed of being pulled

Fearless

by the cruise ship.

Brian quickly woke up Riley and told him that Mr. Daly would be with them shortly. It was the first time I observed some concern from the men when in Mr. Daly's presence.

Fortunately, Mr. Daly only wanted the sailboat to be unhitched. He did not want to return to the ship.

They all laughed and continued to joke about the hilarious situation involving the rough waters, the sailboat, the lack of food, and the urgent need to return. Brian wanted pictures of him holding the briefcase to show loyalty to Mr. Daly. "I want to present evidence of my dedication," he laughingly stated.

"Where's Mike going with that bucket?" I noticed Mike and asked Riley as the boat continued its rocky jerking while passing over each wave. Riley stayed close to me in the kitchen area to help me stay on my feet. We were both trying to stop the dishes and bottles from sliding back and forth and from being thrown around the boat. It all seemed funny, and we laughed even harder.

Mike appeared from the engine room. "The engine is smoking," he announced. We began to smell gas. Laughing, Riley announced that we were full of tuna and fish did not eat full people. We laughed even more.

Mike looked puzzled and returned to the engine room with a bucket of water from the kitchen sink.

Riley continued, "Also, bodies float to shore, so we'll get a decent burial and won't be buried at sea."

We all roared, except for Adella. She opened the can of tuna, and we were served tuna sandwiches with mustard.

I thought of the Bible stories of Jesus feeding the multitudes with the three small fish and the bread.

We then, in the middle of eating, heard a voice from the engine room, "The boat is on fire!" Riley yelled back, "Head the mother to shore!" I fell from the rocking boat to the floor, attempting to move from the kitchen area. "Hang loose," Riley gave his rendition of how to handle the situation. The crew seemed to have become serious. For us, it was just another opportunity to laugh.

Riley continued to laugh and comment, "Joan, let's go in style. Let's make love while the boat is sinking." Brian looked at us in disgust.

Tears of laughter were streaming down my face.

We finally arrived back to shore on a very sick *African Queen*. However, the trip was one I will never forget.

I accompanied Mr. Daly on many of his ventures

around the island for the rest of my time there. The major controversy surrounding Ed Daly was his involvement in the Vietnam airlifts to save the Vietnamese children from the Viet Cong. It appeared that one of the major problems with the United States Government was that Mr. Daly broke bureaucratic rules when he flew his planes into Vietnam to remove the orphan children immediately before the Viet Cong invaded. During his many flights, the plane was overtaken by soldiers who were pushing the children aside and trying desperately to save themselves. The airway was trampled and children were crushed as men pushed women and children out of the way to board the planes themselves. In one particular instance, Mr. Daly stood on the steps of his plane attempting to board women and children. A soldier caught him by the bottom of his pants, almost removing them in his attempt to board the plane. The plane finally took off with the man hanging onto the wheel. He was crushed. Out of 150 people on the plane, only six were women and children. American soldiers shot at the plane as it took off. All in all, Mr. Daly removed more than 10,000 children from combat areas during that war.

Mr. Daly was indeed wealthy. He funded these trips out of his personal funds. Before leaving the Daly party, I went with Mr. Daly to the home of the Cardinal. We were given a tour of the grounds, and I was able to see the home of the aged and the magnificent chapel financed by Ed

Daly. I returned to New York after a wonderful extra week in Apia while singing on the *African Queen*, swimming in the Pacific Ocean, and generally hanging out with the President of World Airways, a man worth more than $30 million! All of this was because, at the right time and under the right circumstances, I had the courage to say YES.

"Do not grieve, for the joy of the Lord is your strength."

- Nehemiah 8:10

Chapter XVII
Giving

The hustle and bustle of New York City gets one right back into the mode of involvement and purpose. I still needed to find ways of connecting. I gradually became involved in other organizations such as The Founding Chapter of One Hundred Black Women, The Mount Morris Community Improvement Association, the Harlem Commonwealth Council, and finally, the one I enjoyed the most – where I worked the hardest and felt more at home – The Harlem Congregations for Community Improvement (HCCI). In fact, I felt so much at home that I sat on the Board without realizing it for 18 years. I actually grew older, wiser, and more focused while serving the community through this Board, and I enjoyed all of it. If one genuinely concentrates on the work, the enjoyment of the work can be felt effortlessly, and it will automatically leave a mark and a legacy. One does not need to focus on the legacy; it comes with the love and enjoyment.

Delta Sigma Theta was in my blood from my days at Southern University. I was also one of the Charter Member of the Baton Rouge Sigma Chapter, which was organized after I finished Southern University. I had forgotten this until I was reminded by a member cousin, Betty's daughter,

Karen. As she put it, "You are the only living charter member of the Baton Rouge Chapter," something that I had totally forgotten. It was a big deal with Karen. It should have been a big deal for me as well, but then it takes time to realize that accomplishments viewed by others is life's passion to you. You do not realize until later that you are doing something that will impact the lives of those who follow you. Then I remembered, as a young Southern University student who had pledged to join the Alfa Tau Chapter of Delta Sigma Theta, how we were required to recognize the charter members of Delta. Dr. Dorothy Height was one of the charter members and a name that I have never forgotten. I remembered the impression I had of her as a person was of an individual of great significance.

I went to several meetings with Karen upon visiting home in Baton Rouge. The young women were so gracious, providing special seating, gifts, and even a special red, draped chair parked right in the middle of the Southern University Alumni designated meeting building. The President gave me a gift bag, and I actually felt great pride for and among the young women who surrounded me. They were all gifted souls who were massively talented and doing great things for the community in Baton Rouge. Youth is wonderful! I could see in their eyes their hopes, dreams, and aspirations. I prayed that those dreams would be fulfilled for each of them. They really honored their "only living charter members," as they described me.

Fearless

New York was different, though. Or maybe New York wasn't what was different – perhaps it was me. I was busy adjusting to an entirely new environment and setting. However, my organizational life in Harlem did lead to one significant decision in my life.

Through a friend, I was led to become a foster mother. For me, it had more meaning and more immediacy for the recipients. I received a call one night that two little four-year-old twin girls needed a home. Unable to say no, I took them for what I thought would be two weeks. Those two weeks were expanded to about ten years. The girls, Lisa and Tiffany, became integral members of my family. They increased the family, both immediate and extended. I take my hat off to my granddaughter, Nikki, for her utmost patience and love. Although only a few years older, Nikki became their mentor, teaching them the basics about childhood, a missing element in their lives. Nikki knew how to connect with the twins in a way that helped me tremendously. Through play, and under Nikki's tutelage, the twins learned to dance, sing, and just have fun. All of the qualities were natural for Nikki. The twins are now grown and on their own. However, I still consider them to be my children.

My house in Harlem was open to all family members, whether they hailed from Louisiana or any other part of the country. They came to study, attend medical school, work,

or visit for extended periods. They came to go to the US Open games, or they came to get away from home. I accepted them all. They were welcome and stayed as long as they wished. After all, they were family.

The exciting thing about Harlem was that it was a "sleeper." Although in my travels and other communities, Harlem had a reputation for being an unsafe place to visit, I found in my neighborhood and the Harlem community in general a very stable and secure middle and upper-class community of African American families. For example, my neighbors owned a brownstone with several original Tiffany-stained windows and lamps in the dining room. The husband was a social worker, and his wife was a nurse. Another family that lived a few blocks over consisted of a doctor and his wife, who were married for more than 40 years. Their daughter was a Broadway dancer and a dance instructor to many children in the neighborhood. There were many such families living in Harlem. Usually, they were the first or second-generation owners of their beautiful homes. Several Broadway dancers, costume and stage designers, and other artists lived with family, parents, and other family members in family-owned dwellings in Harlem. Brownstone owners worked as doctors, social workers, nurses, and other professionals in the medical field.

Harlem Hospital was considered a training center for

interns from the islands and other parts of the country. Harlem was and still is loaded with active and productive professional people living extremely affluent lifestyles. Certain parts of Harlem had an established reputation for affluence. Riverside Drive, Striver's Row, Mount Morris Park, Graham Court, the Morris Jumel Mansion, built in 1765, and its neighboring buildings are a part of the Jumel Terrace Historic District. City College is an anchor in Harlem and always has been. Columbia University is a Harlem institution. There are many other historical examples of affluence. Harlem is now my home after being in New York for more than ten years. I am a hybrid, belonging to Harlem and Baton Rouge.

As though it had happened overnight, I was no longer the young woman relocating from Baton Rouge to New York. I have finally reached a point in life where I can admit that I am a senior citizen who is now very active in the community of Harlem. I hold the title of the First Woman Chairperson of one of the most important organizations in Harlem. I have many acquaintances and a few good friends, engaging with the various elected and appointed officials who held key positions in New York. I am happy, and I even feel somewhat accomplished.

It didn't just happen overnight, though.

My journey is not devoid of disappointments,

dishonesty, and chauvinism, but I never let go of the core principles either. They have always been with me, embedded in my soul and immovable. There are lessons of disappointment that lie in people who do not say what they mean. And then there are people who do not live up to the projections forecasted. There are also disappointments in myself. My much older self thinks about things I could have changed when I was younger that would have made significant differences in my life, at least and maybe in the lives of others. This is where determination steps in. This determination continues to give me the courage to move ahead regardless of disappointments and obstacles because there is and should be tremendous joy in life.

Working as a member of the Board of HCCI was one of the most rewarding and fulfilling experiences in my life in Harlem. I found the ministers to be, for the most part, caring and compassionate. I served on the Board, learning the ins and outs of real estate development and building an environment of community empowerment that was rich and filled with nuggets for a victorious life. I never realized that I served on that Board for 18 years of my life. I grew older while on that Board without any realization whatsoever. I just continued to grow with it. I saw several Chairs of the Board come and go. I saw Board members come and go. I saw many community and homeless people housed, people fed and cared for by community workers. I saw desolation turn into housing for residents of Harlem. So, I was

honored when the Chairman of the Board asked me to consider following him as Chair after he stepped down. I would be the first woman to hold that office. After some deliberation and discussion, I agreed to one year of service as the Chairperson of HCCI. That one year stretched into three additional great years.

When the current Chairman first asked me to serve, I refused his offer. I had misgivings about my capacity to serve in this role. Being the Chair of a Board of African American ministers, primarily from Harlem, and mainly men, left me with some reservations about respect. After all, some ministers do not allow women in the pulpit. Others think women should not be ministers at all, regardless of the fact that upon His rising from the dead, the first person who was sent by Jesus to tell the people about him was a woman. Men have been in the leadership for a very long time. They would not accept a woman at the helm without a fight. *Would they want to listen to me? Would they respect my opinions?* I often pondered. They would have to get accustomed to a woman as Chair, and I had to muster up the courage to provide the organization's leadership and direction of the organization with the assistance of primarily male ministers. Even with a couple of women for support, I did not see that as an easy task.

I laid out my concerns to the then-Chairman, and he assured me that I had already gained the respect and

dedication of the Board members. His words of comfort and assurance eased my concerns, increasing my respect for him as a minister and a man. In other words, with his quirky sense of humor, his human frailties, and his no-nonsense way of getting things done, he understood the issue and was willing to "push the envelope."

The Chairman expressed that it was important that a woman should follow him. "This organization is in its 30th year of serving the community. It is time they had a woman as Chairman," he stated. "I think that you should be that woman." I am thankful that he trusted me. He did query me about many issues, both personal and professional. We disagreed on some of those issues. However, working in partnership with the Board of Directors, we made significant accomplishments. I was also honored when the Board held a surprise party for me upon leaving, where a newly developed building for seniors was unveiled, named, and dedicated to me. I ACTUALLY HAVE A BUILDING NAMED AFTER ME IN HARLEM. Thank you, HCCI.

"DO IT SCARED?!"

"Give, and it shall be given unto you, good measure, shaken together and running over, will be poured into your lap. For with the measures you use, it will be measured to you."

- Luke 5:38

Chapter XVIII
Understanding

I have gone through several trials and tragedies as I continued to grow older. Those hard times have taught me to focus on maintenance as opposed to the one-time flightiness of youth and the ignoring of pain – physical, mental, and emotional – "because it will go away." Pain, both physical and emotional, no longer goes away without some attention to the cause. It probably never did. It becomes necessary to have a "primary care" physician, possibly a counselor, or at least a good friend who is not judgmental. It's also important that there is no stigma attached to any of these service providers and friends. The challenge is finding friends who are not judgmental because that is not easy. There is a very thin line between being judgmental and giving advice and help through wisdom and wishing the best for a friend. Judgment breeds insecurity, while true friendship breeds confidence and guidance toward success and wellness, both physical and mental.

I find it interesting how physical and psychological changes occur gradually but sometimes become a permanent part of our journey.

It becomes necessary for some to have many ancillary

physicians, such as a gynecologist, a dermatologist, a cardiologist, an internal medical doctor, a physical therapist, and for some, even more health service providers: a psychologist, a psychiatrist, a neurologist, a urologist, an orthodontist and all of their related "gists," a pain specialist, and numerous other "gists." If you are a woman, then these people are extremely important in your life. If you are an African American woman, then you had better not only have these people in your life but develop a checklist to make sure you are getting the healthcare you deserve.

In New York, some of these were added to my arsenal of living a healthy and productive life as I moved farther and farther into that phenomenon called "becoming a senior." As I moved through this wonderful blessing of living, I became even more aware of the reality of "ageism," especially for African American women. Sexism, I knew. Racism, I knew. However, ageism was new and thriving. I had to learn and conquer another issue related to being a "single African American senior woman." Ageism does not replace the other two "isms." It only forces itself into one's psyche with all the others. The psychological aspect of all this is dealing with each encounter without losing the joy of life.

I am still in the process of dealing with and sometimes conquering both psychological and physical pain.

Fearless

After a fall in New York, the reality of dealing with physical and psychological pain showed me first-hand how it goes.

Leaving an uptown HCCI meeting with colleagues, I got off the bus to walk to Citi Bank on 125th Street in Harlem. I was in a slight hurry to get the two blocks to the bank. In an attempt to get some daily walking into my schedule, I decided to walk from 8th Avenue across 125th Street as opposed to taking another bus. Walking briskly, I passed several vendors on 125th St. Suddenly, I found myself thrust forward as my foot hit something on the street near the curb. I could not stop my head and shoulders going forward as my feet were stopped by that "something" on the sidewalk. I was headed for a sure fall, with no way of bracing myself. My bag went one way, my shoe was somehow off my right foot, and my head was destined for a collision with the upcoming sidewalk. My arms automatically moved forward to brace the fall, and I landed with my mouth, head, left knee, and shoulders crashing into the sidewalk cement.

I don't remember getting up on my own. However, a man was holding my hands and moving me toward a chair. "You must sit down," he said.

"I have to get to the bank," I replied.

"You cannot go anywhere," he insisted.

"I'm ok," I stated.

"Is there someone I can call?" he asked. "Who can I call?" he repeated.

I gave my daughter's name and contact number. I sat for a few minutes and then got up again to continue my trip to the bank, only to realize that I needed to sit back down. My legs seemed a bit shaky. The man was on his phone calling someone. We were in front of a health center next to a children's shop. He told me that I needed to clean my face. I moved to the health center and went into the bathroom. I was shocked when I looked in the mirror and saw that my face was covered in blood. I had no idea where the blood was coming from. As I came out of the empty health center, the man insisted that I get into the ambulance he had called. I did.

The ambulance attendant wanted to know which hospital I wanted to go to. I asked him which one was the quickest, still thinking about my bank appointment. He said, "Harlem Hospital. You'll be there at least four or five hours before they see you." On that response, I ended up at Lenox Hill Hospital. I was still feeling no pain, but the attendant seemed alarmed. Maybe it was the amount of blood that was now appearing on my clothes.

Once reaching Lenox Hill Hospital, the pain slowly caught up with the blood on the rest of my body. My arm

and shoulder were beginning to ache with pain. My left knee hurt, and my mouth seemed to have difficulty forming words. I was a mess.

As I lay in a cubby, surrounded by a curtain of soft blue flowers hanging from an oval-shaped circular silver pipe-like railing, gradually, the pain began its tour of what seemed to be my entire body. It slowly and increasingly intensified as it engulfed most of my body. My back, legs, and shoulder appeared to be the major points of interest. However, at times, I was not sure what was hurting more. Even Novocain did not help. After several X-rays, prodding, and poking, I was released to go to my physician. It was still four or five hours before I was released from Lenox Hill Hospital.

A day after the fall, I woke up to such excruciating pain that I could hardly walk. My back and legs refused to work properly. I immediately did an exercise taught to me by my physical therapist. I remembered, "Place your hands on the dresser in front of you. Then, step back so that you are leaning over at the waist. Slowly move forward to a standing position and then back to the leaning position by walking slowly backward." The kinks and the pain seemed to subside, but only to return to standing. "Do it at least twelve times in sets of twos." I did that and felt somewhat better. I realized that one may not bounce back as soon as expected when one is younger.

This was not my first time having back pain, even though this pain was different in a way I could not explain. Previously, I found that when I gained weight, my back hurt. I found that when I was anxious about something, my back hurt. The doctors liked to call it arthritis. I did not understand or like that term and always refused to accept it as a condition that came with aging, which the doctors seemed to associate the condition with. I knew too many older women who moved without pain or restrictions. I was never examined for arthritis, only almost always pronounced by doctors that I had it when they were not sure what was going on.

I could not accept a condition that was not visible to the eye, invisible on an X-ray or on an MRI, or any of the other ways they diagnose conditions for older women. I rather thought of it as another symptom of convenience for the doctors' explanation for being older and, in my case, being an African American woman. Arthritis was not like a slipped disk, a broken arm, a bleeding problem, a bruised leg, or a bunion that one could see. It was this invisible condition that came with aging. The same body, only older, was somehow destined to accept this strange invisible pain with no source, time frame, conditions for existence, or way of getting rid of it. When the doctors did X-rays, they pointed to small pockets of what looked like fat and sometimes changed the diagnosis to "just a little" or some other way of identifying the condition.

Fearless

I had a friend who constantly referred to it as "Arthur." She would say, "Wherever I go, Arthur is always there with me."

I asked her, "Who is Arthur?" I thought she had a new man in her life.

A vast number of people that I have encountered loved to talk about their "Arthur." It seemed a badge of honor for lack of exercise, overeating, and numerous other habits resulting in stiffness and pain associated with aging. It appears to me that doctors accept obesity as a condition of existence, especially for more than half of the people who are living with obesity. In fact, they accept it without resistance, even more so when it is related to the African American population, both young and old.

Fat shaming is wrong and judgmental, and that is not what I intend to do here. Good health is necessary and should be available to all through healthcare providers.

Not being a medical doctor, I believe there *is* something called arthritis. However, I refuse to believe it comes and goes. It's either there or it's not. If one doctor can see it, it should be visible to any doctor and to me with the right equipment.

I am always somewhat anxious about going to doctor's appointments. My blood pressure seems to register higher

than its usual 120 to 130 over 70, and I am reminded that I may be a little overweight for my small body frame. No, not by the nurse, attendant, or doctor; it's my own assessment when I routinely "step up on the scales," a process that one must undergo. Whatever number appears on the scale is quickly recorded to go into the archives of history, never to be seen again until the next doctor's visit. However, I see it and am reminded that I should not have had that caramel ice cream with chocolate cake two nights in a row.

When I go in, I am led back into a private room. After waiting for a while, someone comes in and introduces themselves, shows you where to put your things, and proceeds to look over your chart. This person is usually an intern, a student, or someone new to the job with very little experience. They always make sure to cover all of the bases and check all the boxes. After going over every medication you have had since birth, they then check for every surgery, disease, pain, habit, smoking, drugs, sexual preference, and any other potential activity that may compromise your "normal" daily living in any way.

The next step is a bit of an analysis. What is drinking a little? "You've had a lot of surgeries." You listen, not knowing how to answer that. *Maybe it's because I have lived a long time, and some were just trendy at the time.* For example, many years ago, I had my appendix removed.

I also had a cesarean to deliver one of my children. I think that one was necessary, but at this point, I'm not sure. I had a cyst removed, and I had a bunion taken off my big toe. It was not necessary, and my shoes still hurt on the foot that had the bunion. I thought those were necessary, but maybe they weren't.

While she was looking at my history and my medication, she took my blood pressure. "It's too high." *I guess it is*, I thought, after listening to my history of slowly losing body parts through the years.

"Are you taking your blood pressure medicine?" She continued.

"Yes, I am."

"Make sure you continue your statins; it keeps your heart safe."

I thought of my heart. It is the one organ that assures you of life as long as it keeps beating. I guess I had better take those statins daily, not the way I had been taking them; I was taking them occasionally. I decided to take them regularly.

"If you don't take it regularly, it does not work," she added and continued, "You want to protect your heart. Statins keep those little pockets of plaque from seeping into

various parts of your body."

I imagined the little bits of cement and other thick objects lurking throughout my body, looking for a place to snuggle and make themselves comfortable. "Okay," I assured her. I bet if she had checked my blood pressure again, it would have been through the roof. The thought of those little creatures looking for a home in my body really alarmed me.

She suddenly looked at me and seemed surprised at my appearance, "Oh, I asked about the surgeries because I thought you were in your sixties. What is your secret?"

"The grace of God," I answered as usual. This is my standard answer since this question is frequently asked by anyone who suspects me of being younger than the numbers that I had racked up through the years. Don't get me wrong; I love the fact that I look a lot younger than my actual age. Maybe I have some "Benjamin Button" blood. I guess there is something to not acting your age, joyfulness, and a sense of humor as your routine way of living. Maybe youthful dressing and continuing to flirt harmlessly attracted youthful countenance. I accepted and embraced it as my way of life.

Maybe we should look into getting rid of the "you are supposed to act a certain way when you are considered aging" mindset. This should be so, especially if you are a

woman, and even more so if you are an African American woman. I felt a bit better, at least knowing that despite missing parts, plaque wandering around throughout my body, and my heart trying to push cement aside so that it could receive a bit of necessary blood, I still looked much younger than the increasing numbers that were assigned to me each year after birth.

Thank God, on this particular occasion, the doctor came in and announced that the test results were normal and that I should see him in another year. I went home from the hospital and started therapy and pain management at Johns Hopkins and continued to work indirectly on things that made me feel worthy of being a woman, such as losing weight and trying to look younger than my age, which surprisingly came NATURALLY.

> *"It wasn't your word that healed them, but your word alone, Lord which heals everything."*
>
> – Solomon 16:12

Chapter XIX
Life

It doesn't matter if it's New York or any other place, networking is something that truly makes a difference. We get a chance to learn from others through networking, as we should. Besides, networking proves itself as a process of discovery that enables us to learn, develop, and grow. It allows us to discover a world rich in diversity of people and thought.

I am the type of mother who taught her children by example with a few words of guidance thrown in here and there. I love them unconditionally. As I reflect, I could have done a better job. I guess any mother probably feels the same – or at least I hope that is the case anyway. Too bad children don't come with a guidebook! I am the mother of an extremely bright son and a feisty and accomplished daughter. I am the mother of a witty, sharp, and intellectually gifted son. I am a grandmother to a remarkably gifted young woman, Nikki, and a great-grandmother to a blossoming young man, Taymar. My guidebook was crafted for them in the customs, folkways, and morays of Essen Lane. Even more importantly, my mother and grandfather, who introduced me to Jesus Christ at an early age.

Fearless

Children today need to know their legacy. They need to know their roots. The nutrients of a plant come from the seed, and the seed lies in the roots. This alone is enough to express the significance of roots, a place of one's origin. We are the keepers of the legacy, the history, and the roots of our one large family. It is up to us to ensure that our history is passed on to our children.

When I moved slowly on the dance floor to Curtis Mayfield many years ago, he spoke to me, and it became a legacy in his moaning and grunts as he belted out, *"Keep on pushing, some way, somehow, cause I've got my pride, I've got my strength, and it don't make much sense, not to keep on pushing. Hallelujah, keep on pushing. Because someday you will reach your higher goal."*

Here's what I have to say to my daughter, my son, my granddaughter, my great-grandson, my family, and others. So, listen:

"Don't you turn back.

Don't get up and sit down on the steps 'cause you find it's kinda hard.

Don't you fall now, for I am still climbing, and life for me ain't been no crystal stair.

I learned it that we are never alone. We serve a God

who will not leave us, so keep pushing. He's right here with you."

I guess my purpose throughout my career was the children, but it did not start off that way. My first challenge was to make my own money. But then, faced with the young, innocent people, I found the humanity in them to be a drawing factor. They infiltrated my life in a way that I longed to see them succeed. I later added the young women and men as I matured and my children became older. The challenges they began to face became more and more difficult, but not insurmountable. We can do all things through Christ, who strengthens us. Truth became lies, and lies became truth. Theory became fact, no longer needing to be examined or proven. There began a series of events that led to generations of people feeling insecure about all around them as they attempted to establish themselves in a confusing and convoluted world where up is down and down is up.

I only added these people to my quest because I had faced the same challenges, even before I let myself admit it. As I grew older, my awareness expanded to include the status of my own being. So, my thoughts were relative and constantly changing, but always involving the African American people and the challenges we face, especially the young people who are sometimes without guidance or a sense of direction.

Fearless

Sometimes, one gets to a place in life where things are unclear and scattered. I am blessed to be in a position where I am capable of moving forward despite the appearance of obstacles and setbacks.

I wondered what life would hold as one got older. I now know. I came to New York filled with the excitement of youth and adventure and met many great people and some not-so-great but well-meaning, I guess. I tend to believe that all people are well-meaning. I took advantage of everything New York City offered. My advantage lay in the theatres, the nightclubs, Lincoln Center, Radio City Music Hall, the Four Seasons, the Brasserie, and, of course, uptown at Under the Stairs, the Blue Note, Smalls Paradise, and all the others. I was even driven home by "Bumpy Johnson" in a limo from one of those places. I believed him when he told me he was in the extermination business, and I am pretty sure now that he was.

My life has been about doing things for others, sometimes instead of doing things for myself. I think I learned better, but I am not sure I have. Sometimes, I still do it for others instead of myself. It is not because I am so altruistic but because I don't like the look of disappointment from others and because it reflects on their feelings about me. So, it's still about me in the end.

Although I grew up in my grandfather's small Baptist

Church, I did not really understand all of what being a Christian entailed. I did not understand how to lean on the word of God to change my life. Challenges throughout my life have changed that. I know that without a stable belief in and reliance on Jesus, there is no victory. When Yvonne was banging out a song on the piano during our teen years, we also included some Christian songs. Those are still with me. Songs such as "Amazing Grace" and "What a Friend we have in Jesus" are some that are still with me, along with the blues we loved so well. My strength comes from them and their all-encompassing meaning.

Langston Hughes spoke to me and probably many other mothers in his *Mother to Son* message when I found myself in melancholy moments. And then there was Curtis Mayfield, who spoke to me when I reminisced about the times I was dancing in little smoky nightclubs and learning to drink bourbon and coke with my husband. I still chose not to turn around.

We are filled with potential of which we are unaware. "Where there is a will, there is a way," I heard my mother's voice in my head. Mother told me as I brought her lunch one day, "You have a strong will." We would laugh a lot together, she and I. We would laugh at issues, people, even objects, and ourselves. We believed that life, in general, was funny, so we laughed. Our joy was complete. I learned from her that despite setbacks, there is always joy to be

had, laughter to experience, and diamonds to be discovered and possessed. So, we must not turn back. Where would we go? Besides, the crystals and diamonds are ahead of us and they are plentiful if we just look around and gather them and, by the way, TAKE THE ELEVATOR!

"But let patience have her perfect work, that ye may be perfect and entire, wanting nothing."

– James 1:4

Made in the USA
Columbia, SC
05 July 2024

fd8f269c-77b7-45b8-b6e9-6710a1c78dfeR01